Entrepreneur®
MAGAZINE'S

start up

Start Your Own

HERB AND HERBAL PRODUCTS BUSINESS

*Your Step-by-Step
Guide to Success*

Rob and Terry Adams

Editorial Director: Jere L. Calmes
Managing Editor: Marla Markman
Cover Design: Beth Hansen-Winter
Production: Eliot House Productions
Composition: Patricia Miller

This publication is designed to provide accurate and authoritative information in regard to the subject matter covered. It is sold with the understanding that the publisher is not engaged in rendering legal, accounting or other professional services. If legal advice or other expert assistance is required, the services of a competent professional person should be sought.

Library of Congress Cataloging-in-Publication Data

Adams, Rob, 1950–
    Start your own herb and herbal products business/by Rob and Terry Adams.
        p.   cm.   —(Entrepreneur magazine's start up) (Entrepreneur magazines's business start-up series; #1282)
    Includes index.
    ISBN 1-932156-02-X
    1. Herb industry—Management. 2. New business enterprises—Management.
I. Title: Herb and herbal products business. II. Adams, Terry, 1952– III. Title. IV. Series. V. Series:Entrepreneur business start-up guide; no. 1282.

HD9019.H472 A33 2003
635'.7'068—dc21   2002192845

Printed in Canada

09 08 07 06 05 04 03   10 9 8 7 6 5 4 3 2 1

Contents

Chapter 11

Plant People:
Dealing with Customers and Employees 131

Chapter 12

Growing Your Business:
Advertising and Marketing 141

▲

Preface

Y
ou've chosen this book because you've got the seed of a very exciting idea: You're planning to start an herb business. You'll be living the dream of countless thousands of people—to get back to nature, coax new growth from seed and soil, even craft products from your own herbs and be your own boss.

In these days when so many of us are 9-to-5ers who march to the beat of a corporate drum, farming and crafting is an exciting proposition. But it can also be a scary one. While you'll be your own boss, you're not the boss of Mother Nature. You'll have to work with, or despite, heat and cold, frost, flood, storm, and drought. And then there are those bossy types like the IRS, the FDA, and your local agriculture and health departments to contend with. When you're in charge of the farm, you can't turn to someone else to handle questions, problems, and concerns—you're it.

But you're also the one who gets to make all the decisions, bask in the warmth of the sun, inhale the sweet scent of fresh herbs, and work (as so many earlier generations have done) at crafting the fruits of your labors into products others can enjoy. You'll be earning a living at something you love, and that's priceless.

You're probably considering becoming an herbal entrepreneur for one or more of the following reasons:

- You love gardening and farming and making things grow.
- You've fallen for the romance and mystique of herbs.
- You enjoy making and selling craft products.
- You have a background in farming or horticulture and feel this would be an excellent way to combine your experience with a satisfying new business and lifestyle.
- You believe the herb industry is flourishing, and you're eager to share in the excitement and willing to take a chance on success.

Which did you choose? It doesn't matter: Any of these responses is entirely correct so long as you realize that *this business involves a lot of learning and a lot of hard work.* It can also involve a heck of a lot of fun, as well as a tremendous amount of personal and professional satisfaction.

Our goal here is to tell you everything you need to know to:
- decide if an herb business is right for you;
- get your farm and your business up and running; and
- make your farm a success.

We've attempted to make this book as user-friendly as possible. We've interviewed lots of people on the front lines of the herb industry—all around the country—to learn the nitty-gritty of the tips and tricks to a successful herb business. You'll hear them tell their own stories and give their own hard-won advice, as well as suggestions that place you right in the thick of things. We've broken our chapters into manageable sections on every aspect of start-up, production, and promotion and packed our pages with helpful tips so that you can get up and running on your new herb farm as quickly as possible. We've also provided an appendix crammed with contacts and sources. Best of all, we've left some space for your creativity to soar.

So pour a giant mug of herb tea, take a deep breath, turn off the television, set your brain to learning mode, and let's go!

1

The Dirt on Herb Farming
What's It All About?

Herbs are in these days. Everywhere you look, you find them in one form or another. Herbs star in gourmet cuisine at swanky restaurants, they put in regular appearances in the fresh produce section of supermarkets, and greet you on drugstore shelves. They soothe, scent, and stimulate the senses in potpourri, candles, body lotions, and bath products.

They are increasingly featured not only in the remedies of home-health providers like Dr. Mom, but also in the recommendations of a growing number of medical professionals. And, of course, gardeners look to herbs for their easy growing habits and aromatic qualities.

But herbs aren't anything new. They've been prized as cosmetics, medicines, and foodstuffs for thousands of years, long before written languages began recording their uses. Herbalism—mostly in a medicinal context—was practiced from China to North America, the Mediterranean and the Middle East. During the Middle Ages, European monks kept the secrets of herbs alive by copying *herbals*—detailed herb treatises with illustrations—that served as medical texts and minding "physick" gardens filled with medicinal herbs. Centuries later, herbs took a back seat to modern medicine and cooks abandoned fresh herbs in favor of modern—if flavorless—convenience foods.

Photo© PhotoDisc Inc.

A Little Romance

Now that we've arrived at the new millennium, however, herbs are back in favor in a big way. People the world over have rediscovered their romance, mystique, and allure. But what exactly is this fascination? Why are we suddenly so taken with plants—most of which are essentially weeds—that have been around since long before humans wandered onto the scene?

"Herbs are especially important to us today, I believe, for both real and symbolic reasons," says Susan Wittig Albert, a noted herbalist, columnist for *The Herb Companion* magazine, and author of a popular series of mystery novels that prominently features herbal tips and lore. "They offer useful culinary, medicinal, landscaping, crafting, and decorating possibilities. At the same time, they represent a connection to a bountiful earth and to our human past, and suggest a healthy and sustainable lifestyle. In our complicated, highly technologized society, we cherish herbs because they seem somehow right and simple."

In a world that seems to be spinning ever faster, tantalizing us with technical wonders while threatening to forever leave the lifestyles of our grandparents, our parents, and even ourselves in the dust, herbs help us tune in to nature and forge a link with prior generations of farmers, gardeners, cooks, and healers. There's something ultimately satisfying about rediscovering the secrets of the past and forming a partnership with the natural world in the present.

And everyone, it seems, is in on the trend. Chefs in trendy restaurants and home kitchens demand herbs to enhance flavor and replace blood-pressure-elevating salt. Medical researchers promote herbs as healthy alternatives to costly and dangerous pharmaceuticals. Makers of bath and beauty products infuse their goods with herbs both for their scents and therapeutic qualities. And everybody buys herbal teas, candles, potpourri, and other aromatic essences for those same therapeutic qualities... all of which makes the business of herbs an exciting and rewarding one.

Herbs for All Seasons

Herbs exert a magic that infuses some people inside and out. Once they've discovered the tastes and scents and dipped into the ancient lore, they're hooked. If you're one such herb aficionado, what could be better than a business in which herbs are an integral essence? You can grow them; buy them; sell them; craft with them; decant lotions, potions, bath salts, and vinegars; package herbal oils and mixes for cooking; and teach classes on growing and using herbs.

Good Medicine

As part of the herbal renaissance, the medical and pharmaceutical communities have already discovered—much to their own surprise—that much of the ancient lore of "physick" gardens has a basis in solid reality. Herbs are good for you!

In Germany, a concentrated form of St. John's wort, a shrubby herb bearing star-shaped yellow flowers, has been prescribed by doctors for depression for years and is the most prescribed drug on the market. According to GardenGuides.com, one report showed that German physicians wrote 200,000 prescriptions for a single brand of hypericum (the Latin name for St. John's wort) compared with only 30,000 prescriptions for a single brand of its pharmaceutical counterpart, fluoxetine, or Prozac.

In the United States, doctors have been much slower to advocate St. John's wort over Prozac. But walk into any pharmacy in the country (as well as any supermarket's pharmacy section), and you'll see a wide variety of bottled hypericum capsules lining the shelves.

You'll also see echinacea, or purple coneflower, in capsules and even in cough drops. This common herb was widely used by American Indians, and apparently so effectively that European settlers spirited its seeds back to their homelands to make sure they'd have the plant in constant supply. As part of our herbal renaissance, echinacea is once again in common use as a cold- and flu-buster.

Stat Fact

Sales of greenhouse and nursery crops, including cut and potted flowers, bedding plants, and cut cultivated greens—all part of the herb revolution—rose 34 percent in a recent seven-year period, according to the U.S. Census Bureau.

Herbal businesses run the gamut from rural herb farms to sophisticated urban shops—or, surprisingly enough, urban herb farms and rural farm shops, as well as every type of sales venue and location in between. You can sell your herbs freshly harvested, dried, or as potted plants. And you can make and sell all sorts of herbal products, from chip dips and jellies to teas, dream pillows, potpourri, soaps, shampoos, fragrances, candles, wreaths, notecards…and more!

No matter the character and location of your herbal business, you'll most likely want to grow your own plants. A large part of the joy of herbs lies in participating in the magic of the growing season, harvesting their bounty, then nurturing them on to new growth as the seasons turn full circle. Herbal entrepreneurs take pride in owning businesses that allow them to experience life's cycles along with nature and escape claustrophobic workplaces where the only detectable change in seasons is from forced heat to air conditioning and back.

Some entrepreneurs choose raising herbs as a way to get back to the land. In a world where it often seems that computers, fax machines, and voice mail rule, living for sun and rain and the rich texture and scent of fresh earth beneath your fingers can be a powerful magnet. And starting an herb farm—unlike a vineyard, orchard, or coffee plantation—can be a relatively inexpensive way to experience the earth. Herbs are congenial crops; they don't demand much in terms of acreage or special nutrients, so you don't need a big bankroll to get started. And with many popular herbs, you don't have to wait years to harvest your first yields.

Some people opt for herb farming as a way to get out of the rat race—which doesn't necessarily mean leaving the city or the 'burbs. You can successfully grow enough herbs on vacant lots or other fallow land tucked into corners of the area where you live. Plus, while you're still a city dweller, you've escaped the 9-to-5 drudgery of the white-collar world and become not only a farmer, but also your own boss.

Growing an Income

The type of business you choose is a large factor in determining what kind of start-up costs and earnings you can expect. You can sell fresh-cut herbs to restaurants and markets; sell potted plants to garden centers and home gardeners; operate a display garden, retail shop, and restaurant on your farm; or make and sell herbal products from wreaths to body lotions to herb vinegars. You can start as a backyard gardener with a few hundred square feet of growing space or go all out as an agribusiness with several acres.

Whichever you choose, you must go into the business with a plan and monetary goals, cautions Maureen Rogers, president of the Herb Growing and Marketing Network (HGMN) in Silver Spring, Pennsylvania, who's seen lots of would-be farmers fail. It's definitely important, she says, to be a good businessperson as well as an herb lover.

Earning Your Keep

How much can you expect to earn as herb farmer? "It depends on how much time and energy you want to devote," advises Paul Mertel, president of the International Herb Society in Fredericksburg, Virginia. Your annual earnings will vary with factors beyond your control like the season, the weather, and wholesale market prices around the world. As a ballpark range, industry experts suggest that you figure about $5,000 to $30,000 per acre for in-ground crops. The latter figure is for crops that take from three to five years to mature, so your profits won't be immediate.

Keep in mind, too, that these are extremely variable numbers that depend not only on those beyond-your-control factors, but also on elements like what herbs you choose to grow and how savvy and assertive you are in marketing them. And you can add considerable income to these figures if you sell retail potted plants or herbal products in addition to your wholesale items.

Industry experts warn against assuming you can support a family of five (or even two) in the style of rich and famous on an herb farmer's earnings. "In this economy, all small farms have at least one off-farm wage earner," says Rogers.

Risky Business?

Besides earnings and start-up costs, two other factors to consider are risk and stability. Unless you're a heavy-risk gambler type, you don't want a business that's an odds-on favorite to fail. Nor do you want a business that's a fad, destined to shine for only a few brief years, like pet rocks and ant farms, and then fade into thankful (for everyone but you) oblivion.

The verdict on herb businesses is that the risk factor is moderate and the stability rate is good. There's a measure of risk involved with starting any new business, but if you've got a green thumb, you learn to grow and harvest herbs commercially, and you market effectively, you've got a fair chance at success.

And since more and more people, from housewives to health professionals, are discovering the value of herbs every year, the trend seems to be on an upswing—which means herb farms are most likely here to stay.

Mertel agrees. "We find you don't really survive off herbs by themselves," he says. "For most of our members, it's a side business or a second-income business."

Which is not to say that you can't be successful—just that it doesn't happen overnight. "Have patience," advises Michele B., an herb entrepreneur in Soddy Daisy, Tennessee. "It takes time for people to find you, and you can't go out and make them buy from you—not in this business."

"No small flower grower drives a Mercedes or a BMW," counsels Ralph C., who raises herbs and specialty cut flowers in Elizabethtown, Pennsylvania. "It's a lifestyle. You can be comfortable, but rich isn't going to happen." That's fine with Ralph, as it is with all the herb growers we talked with. "It's work," he says. "But it's satisfying to me as a person. This is what I love—it's in my blood."

> ## Smart Tip
> Tip...
>
> Keep in mind that in most parts of the country, herb farming is a seasonal occupation. Unless you have a year-round greenhouse or a way to extend your year with products like dried herbs, you may not have a year-round income.

Seed Money

You can't start counting those profits, however, until you're up and running. And for an herb business—as for any new business—it will cost you a certain amount of seed money to get going. How much, again, depends on exactly what type of operation you plan to run. An herb garden in your existing backyard will be a far less expensive investment than purchasing a full-fledged farm on country acreage. And a simple wholesale business, in which you'll grow and harvest your herbs and then deliver them to buyers around town, will be far less costly to start than an herb farm that includes a retail shop and tea room.

Industry experts suggest you plan for start-up costs of $5,000 to $20,000—assuming you already have your cleared land and a delivery vehicle and that you're considering a simple operation with no retail additions. Your costs are also dependent on whether you already have equipment and are going to tackle the planting and harvesting labor on your own, Rogers explains. If not, your start-up costs will increase.

Raising the Right Stuff

A significant factor to consider in deciding if an herb business right for you is your personality. Not everybody has the right stuff to raise plants for a living or to craft products from them after a day spent weeding, watering, and delivering.

Even though herbs are fairly self-sufficient, they require a lot of care during the growing season. They need watering, weeding, fertilizing, and—if you'll grow them year-round—protection from the elements. You can't suddenly decide to hop on a plane for Hawaii on a whim and leave them unattended. And whether you'll sell wholesale or retail, your customers will expect you to either make deliveries or be in your shop with the doors open during regular intervals.

So if you're a free spirit who's not into being tied to other living things, as well as to routines, you may want to choose another business.

As an herb grower, you'll interact intimately with Mother Nature—even when the temperature soars to 98 in the shade. A lot of what goes into farming is hot, sticky, dirty, and sore-muscle-making. If you're just not a back-to-nature type, no amount of trendy herbal lore is going to make you feel cool, dry, clean, and pleasant. You'll be miserable. But if you're a gardener at heart, you'll be in heaven.

And there's more to it than playing in the dirt. You must also have a savvy business brain. "Successful growers find a niche that's not being met," says the HGMN's Maureen Rogers. "They do not try to be all things to all people. They're all outgoing and like to talk. They get actively involved in trade associations—being on the board, volunteering for committees—because that's where they feel they make the best contacts. In other words, they're very astute business folk, not just farmers."

As you'll see from the following stories, none of the people we interviewed for this book started out as herbal entrepreneurs. Instead, they took their love of herbs and working the land, mixed in the skills and enthusiasm they'd already acquired in prior fields, and changed gears to herb farming.

Dream Come True

"It's always been a dream of mine to grow herbs in a way that would allow me to stay at home, make some money, and just enjoy growing," says Michele B., who with her husband, Scott, owns an herb farm in southeastern Tennessee. "I have always had an herb garden, and I studied herbs for over 15 years. Almost five years ago, we moved to Soddy Daisy and steadily worked to establish the gardens and build the greenhouses. We've been selling our plants for two years now; 18 months ago I was able to quit my day job as a manufacturing secretary.

"We sell our herbs retail. Our primary business is mail order—catalog and Web— but we're also open to the public during growing season. We usually start opening when the weather warms here and pretty much ship plants all year round if the weather permits."

Thanks to a combination of hard work and smart marketing, Michele's dream is a reality. The farm, a moment's drive from Possum Creek and with a wonderful view of the Cumberland Plateau, sits on several acres of forest. "The 12 gardens and two greenhouses sit on a sunny acre with welcome shade from a huge live oak tree," Michele explains. "It's very rural here, but a few minutes' drive, and you're back in civilization."

Down Texas Way

Almost half a continent away, Cindy M. grows herbs Texas-style in Hallettsville, a small town in Hill Country. "Our farm is 158 acres total," Cindy says, "mostly given over to cattle raising and hay and feed crop fields." Of this spread, the herb farm occupies about an acre.

"I have one small greenhouse that I use mostly for seedlings," Cindy explains. "The bulk of my stock is grown outdoors year-round. Because of this setup, certain herbs are only available seasonally. I sell both wholesale and retail. I started out mainly selling wholesale, but since I enjoy customer contact I decided to sell retail as well."

Cindy, who is also vice president of the Texas Herb Growers and Marketers Association, says that she wasn't always a professional herb farmer, even though she lived on a farm. "As my interest in gardening intensified, my attention to a previous home-based business waned," she says. "I wanted to spend more time in my garden and with my plants instead of looking at them from behind a sewing machine inside my workshop. So I closed my clothing business of 18 years and in a few months showed up at a fall festival selling potted herbs—just like that. I have now been at it for about three years. And I'm still learning a lot every season."

In Full Bloom

Up north, in the Amish country of Elizabethtown, Pennsylvania, Ralph C. has 47 acres devoted to decorative fresh and dried herbs, flowers, grains, and grasses. Half of Ralph's business is fresh materials sold to wholesale florists and half is wholesale dried materials sold retail, which includes crafters and gift shops. Ralph also sells unusual seeds, a sideline that constitutes only 5 percent to 7 percent of his farm's income, but is rewarding nonetheless. "It gives you winter work, cleaning and packing seeds," Ralph says. "And it gives me satisfaction to see this stuff get into trade."

Ralph grew up in a family that raised and dried flowers for a living, but he didn't start out to be an herb and flower farmer. He dabbled in dairy farming and ran heavy equipment for a power company—which later proved to be terrific experience in buying and operating farm equipment.

When his parents gave him some leftover plants years ago, Ralph wasn't particularly interested. But he gave it a go and grew them on 1.25 acres as a part-time venture. Then, 15 years ago, Ralph decided to go full time, planting out 10 acres. Now with 47 herb and flower acres—recently featured in *Martha Stewart Living* magazine—he's still in love with the business.

The Accidental Herbalist

In Michigan's upper peninsula, Donna F. sells fresh-cut herbs, edible flowers, dried herb mixes, and herbal vinegars from plants she grows in her backyard garden. Her main growing area measures only about 30 feet by 125 feet, but there are also herbs tucked in amongst the veggies, grapes, apples, pears, and peaches. With assistance from two of her three daughters, Donna sells her products at her local farmers' market two days a week from the beginning of May to the end of October, as well as by mail. She calls on her culinary expertise as a home economics major to develop no-salt herbal mixes that top the taste charts.

The Midland resident got started with herbs 17 years ago when a neighbor who was moving gave her custody of his box of seeds—coincidentally at the beginning of the herbal renaissance in this country. "I planted 23 varieties that spring," Donna says. "I didn't know anything about herbs, but I read and learned, and one thing led to another." She showed up at her first farmers' market with a few bottles of chive blossom vinegar and some herbs, both cut and potted, and expanded from there. She now boasts a line of 35 different dried mixes.

Greener Pastures

On Washington state's Olympic peninsula, Mike and Jadyne R. live among 5 acres of lavender and another $2^1/_2$ acres of assorted herbs grown for their essential oils. Although herb farming has been their life and livelihood for the past five years, Mike and Jadyne—like the other herb growers we talked to—did not start out that way.

Jadyne was a science teacher (she still teaches at a local middle school), and Mike was a state park ranger, which he loved. But as Mike rose through the ranks, he realized he'd become an administrator instead of a hands-on practitioner; the challenge was gone and he was bored. Added to that was the fact that the couple had been living in parks for 15 years and felt it was time to settle down and look for a place to build both a home and some equity.

They found the perfect spot in the Sequim Dungeness Valley. "It was just a big cow pasture," Mike says. He knew there had to be a

Fun Fact

Making a statement in the 8th century that is becoming true again today, King Charlemagne described the herb as "the friend of physicians and the praise of cooks."

use for all that land, but exactly what it was eluded him…until he attended a meeting ("40 middle-aged ladies and me," Mike says) held to persuade local landowners to grow lavender in the Valley's ideal microclimate.

Mike was convinced—and hooked. "I came home and said, 'Jadyne, we're now lavender growers,'" he recalls. The couple researched which varieties of lavender were desirable in the industry and spent three to four years planting them out. "We now have 15,000 plants," Mike says proudly, "a nice big purple haze here on the farm. It was a whimsy and a tremendous risk."

And it paid off. "We're way in the black for the first time," Mike says of the farm's fifth year in business. Its lavender bundles and products—everything from room spritzers and sachets to culinary packets and lavender-filled hair scrunchies—are carried in 800 retail stores, as well as in the farm's own shop. The farm has been featured on Home & Garden Television and in a host of national magazines, and swarms of visitors jostle for attention April through September. "The growing season starts in April with plant sales," Mike explains. "And by June we're going full-boat craziness, flying all over the place." With classes and mail order sales to fill in the gaps, the farm is busy every month of the year.

Herbal Forecast

After you've considered your own personality, as well as the start-up costs and potential profits, one final issue to consider is the forecast for the herb industry. Will herbs as a business be around for the long term, or is the whole herbs for health, beauty, and romance thing a fad that will soon fade?

"The potential is excellent," says Maureen Rogers of the HGMN, "but we're in a shakeout period that will leave many large and small businesses in the dust. The consumer needs more education as to the value of herbs and what to expect from them. The media makes medicinal herbs sound like 'natural' drugs, and the consumer then expects them to act like drugs—providing immediate relief—when that's not how herbs work in the body. This has translated into large inventories of product that are not moving, which means the grower can't expect their normal buyer to be interested.

"The successful farmer is the one that thinks outside the box regarding marketing and does a tremendous amount of networking and research. He's the one you find at a lot of conferences talking to

Stat Fact

According to the National Gardening Association, Americans spent $168 million on herb gardening in a single recent year.

potential buyers in the hall. And he has not only Plan A but Plan B, C, and maybe D, and is very willing to shift gears if necessary."

Texas Herb Growers and Marketers Association vice president Cindy Meredith agrees. "I think the industry future is strong," she says. "Gardening revenue grows each year. More and more people are looking for cleaner, healthier lifestyles, and that includes everything from cooking with fresh herbs to treating menopause symptoms with herbal products. Where a given farmer, retailer, or producer fits in depends on location, desire, and how hard you're willing to work to make your business happen.

"Just because herbs are 'hot' doesn't mean that running any type of herbal-related business is easy. No business is easy; there are no shortcuts. Do your homework, read, talk to people, and be ready to work your tail off; then you might be a success in your chosen business venture."

So what are you waiting for? Brew up a cup of ginseng tea for energy and let's move on!

2

The
Historical Herb
Getting to the Root
of the Matter

You've read Chapter 1 and realize that herbs offer a harvest of satisfaction both personally and financially. You're ready to dig into your farm and set up your workshop. Great! But even though herbs take us back to the basics, there are still a lot of basics to be learned. And the more you know, the more successful your herbal business

▲

will be. So don that sun hat and those gardeners' gloves, and step into the field laboratory for your first lesson in herbs.

The Sands of Time

Herbs and humans have interacted since prehistoric times, which makes sense—people whose existence depended upon what they could gather from the land would learn very early the differences between edible plants and dangerous ones. That in turn would lead them to identify those plants with healing (as well as poisonous) properties. How far back are we talking? Scientists have identified a half-dozen medicinal herbs in a Neanderthal burial site that date back at least 60,000 years.

Since then, herbs have been known and used in medicines, cosmetics, and cooking, and in religious rituals in the ancient China of the emperors, the Egypt of the pharaohs, Biblical Babylon, classical Greece and Rome, the Dark Ages of Europe and its flowering Renaissance, and in native and colonial America... and on into our contemporary world.

Ancient History

One of the earliest recorded herbals was penned more than 3,000 years ago in China by Emperor Shen-nung. Shen-nung was not only a dedicated herbalist, but also an apparently fearless one, using himself as a human guinea pig on whom to test his botanical medicines. Legend has it that the emperor had a transparent stomach that allowed him to view the effects of his herbal preparations on his internal organs up close and personally. While this part of the story is undoubtedly a piece of gruesome, if imaginative, PR, Shen-nung's herbal, the *Pen Tsao*, with its 365 medical remedies—one for each day of the modern year—still exists.

Even older than Shen-nung's herbal remedies is ayurveda, or the science of life, a medical system that according to legend was taught by the gods to the Hindus of ancient India. One of the most famous of the ayurvedic herbals is the *Charaka Samhita*, which lists 500 botanical remedies—although not written down until the first century A.D., thanks to oral tradition it had already been widely used for centuries.

Perhaps as proof that everything old is new again, ayurveda is becoming popular among modern Western herbalists. Like other holistic approaches, ayurveda takes on body and mind as an integrated system—as opposed to modern Western medicine that insists on treating the disease as a separate entity from the sufferer. And, of course, ayurvedism promotes the use of herbs. Take a peek at any herbal magazine, newsletter, or Web site, and you'll see references to the ayurvedic system.

While the Hindus were boning up on ayurvedic medicine, the Egyptians were also delving into the botanical sciences. Terrific chemists, the Egyptians used herbs as the base

What Is an Herb, Anyway?

What makes an herb an herb and not some other sort of plant? The answers vary a bit depending on which experts you ask. The most common definition of an herb is that it's any plant with a fleshy stem that dies back in winter. In other words, trees and shrubs with hardy, woody trunks need not apply. But this answer is not quite complete because trees like the gingko, shrubs like the juniper, and even tough-stemmed roses are considered herbs... as are root crops from homely garlic to exotic Siberian ginseng. So modern herbalists generally agree that an herb is any plant or part of a plant used for its culinary, medicinal, or aromatic qualities.

Not only flowers, but leaves, stems, berries, seeds, roots, and even bark can constitute a plant's listing in the herb roster. Some plants contribute only one usable part, while others provide a bounty of elements for the herbal entrepreneur to harvest and put to use. Add to this the fact that about 10,000 herbs are currently recognized, and you have an incredibly diverse selection with which to work.

for not only medicines, but also cosmetics, perfumes, seasonings, and even fumigation. And, of course, herbs lay at the heart of their most famous botanical art, embalming.

In 1874, long after the pharaohs had disappeared into the sands of time, a German archaeologist, Georg Ebers, discovered an Egyptian herbal dating back to 1550 B.C. Known as the *Ebers Papyrus*, this "book" is actually a 65-foot-long roll of papyrus that lists approximately 800 medicinal herbs, including fenugreek, garlic, and thyme.

Not to be outdone, the Greeks and Romans developed their own herbals, some of which were so popular that they became the standard for European medicine for the next 1,500 years. Hippocrates, well-known as the father of modern medicine, was a learned herbalist. Galen, physician to the emperor Marcus Aurelius, wrote a famous herbal. And Dioscorides, a doctor who tramped about with the Roman legions, penned *De Materia Medica*. This herbal, describing more than 500 botanicals as remedies, is considered by many historians to have been the definitive European "medical text" throughout the Middle Ages and even the Renaissance.

But the Romans contributed much more than medical textbooks. As they traveled throughout Europe, they brought with them—and left behind—a host of Mediterranean herbs and methods for their use in both cooking and healing.

Through the Ages

During the Middle Ages, monks took over as the keepers of herbal knowledge and monasteries sheltered walled gardens filled with botanicals. These carefully cultivated herbs were used as medical remedies, as well as culinary seasonings (important in a world without refrigeration where much of what people ate was—and tasted— spoiled); dyes for clothing and illustrated manuscripts; insecticides against moths, lice, and fleas; and decorative accents for the monastic chapel.

By the time the Renaissance began to bloom, herbs had segued from the monastery to the home, and every lady had her *stillroom*, where she mixed herbal remedies, cosmetics and home-keeping products for her household. Thanks to the invention of the printing press, as well as the brilliance of publishing herbals in plain English instead of Latin, herbs were in such wide use during this period that it's known as the Great Age of Herbals.

Two of the most famous Renaissance-era herbals—to which you'll still find references today—are John Gerard's *Herball*, or *Generall Historie of Plantes*, written in 1597, and Nicholas Culpeper's *Physicall Directory* (1649) and *The English Physician*, otherwise known as *The Complete Herbal* (1651).

Texts such as these tended to offer interesting folkloric tidbits as fact—for instance, that the mandrake root must be gathered only at night and be pulled up by dogs. (Humans who heard the unearthly scream of the plant as it was harvested died instant and agonizing deaths.) But they also presented pharmacological information that today is recognized as scientific fact, such as that lovage has diuretic properties, as well as culinary tips, like how to cook and serve burdock.

When the colonists sailed to the New World and settled in, they brought their herbs with them. Planted in kitchen gardens, they included the same favorites we recognize today, including lavender, parsley, sage, rosemary, thyme, savory, licorice, mint, and basil. They added calendula, madder, and woad to make dyes for coloring clothing, and pot herbs for the cook pot including cress, purslane, and sorrel.

As an added bonus, the European transplants discovered a vast new medicine chest and pantry in the Americas. You may already know that the potato, tomato, and that staple of the sweet-toothed, chocolate, were unheard of in Europe until they were brought back from the New World. But did you know that native North Americans introduced the newcomers to the purple coneflower, or as we know it on our drugstore shelves, echinacea? They also taught the medicinal properties of the willow (which contains salicin, the active ingredient on which aspirin is based) and bee balm (which contains thymol, a potent antiseptic).

Fun Fact

When the colonists tossed the leaves of their favorite beverage into Boston's harbor as a prelude to the Revolution, their American Indian neighbors provided them with a tasty substitute—bee balm, an herb also known as bergamot or Oswego tea. This trendy herb, along with the New Jersey tea plant and a host of other native plants, became known as "liberty teas."

The Synthetic Revolution

As romantic and cozy as the kitchen herb garden appears to us, it didn't provide all the answers for a world that was speeding into the age of technology. Along with the Industrial Revolution and all its attendant wonders, America—and the world—witnessed the Civil War, the First World War, and then the Second—each more horrifying and bloody than the last; each with more wounds to heal and diseases to fight.

So when penicillin first became available in 1943, it was hailed as a miracle drug, as were its antibiotic successors. People had already begun to view herbal medicine as antiquated, and the new wonder drugs only added to this notion.

And while the kitchen, or "victory," garden was an important part of what went on the dinner table in the years before and during World War II, it too faded into the background after the conflict ended. Home cooks fell in love with TV dinners, instant pudding, five-minute grits, Spam, Jell-O, and anything else that came in a can, box, or aluminum foil package. It was quick, easy, and—although flavorless—Space Age and fun! And if you needed more health in your diet, why, you simply popped some vitamins.

Which brings us to the 21st century and the new renaissance of all things herbal. Unlike our predecessors, however, who relied on herb power because they had no other options, we've got the best the ancient and contemporary worlds have to offer.

We can speed through meal preparation with processed foods when we're truly in a hurry and nourish body and soul through the satisfying rituals of cooking with time-honored gifts from the garden when we're not. We can treat the minor ills of ourselves and our families with plants grown by our own hands with the security that all the miracles of modern medicine are available whenever necessary. With supermarkets and drugstores on every corner, we can grow kitchen, victory, and physick gardens for the pleasure they bring rather than because we have to. And we can indulge in bath, beauty, and home fragrance products every bit as luxurious as those enjoyed by pharaohs, emperors, and princesses of old. Who could ask for more?

The Natural Pharmacy

So what exactly is the big deal about herbs as nature's pharmacy? What makes botanicals a viable alternative to all those pills and vials on the drugstore shelves? The answers to these questions are complex enough to fill the pages of dozens of Ph.D.-level biochemistry textbooks, as well as thousands of papers, articles, treatises and popular books. And indeed, you'll find as much reading material on the subject as you can absorb.

To reduce the mass of scientific research and debate to its simplest form, it's important to understand that all medicines originally came from plants. Until the advent of modern chemistry, there wasn't any other source. You may be surprised to learn that even today, 80 percent of the global population looks to herbal remedies as its main health-care option. And if you think this figure is made up of the Third-World residents you see standing barefoot in TV commercials for charitable foundations, you'd be wrong. Approximately 25 percent of the prescription drugs produced in the United States come from plants or are manmade facsimiles of botanical chemicals. And in Europe, especially in Germany, doctors prescribe certain herbs—notably St. John's wort and echinacea—far more frequently than they do their synthetic counterparts.

Nature *vs.* Science

Herbalists, physicians, and medical researchers who believe in the power of phytomedicines, or botanical medicines, point out that many of the components of age-old herbal remedies are in fact medicinal elements commonly recognized by the modern biochemical community.

Ephedra is a good example. Known in China as *ma huang*, it has been cultivated for the past 5,000 years as a treatment for respiratory diseases including asthma. Its American cousin, called Mormon tea, was used by both American Indians and pioneer settlers as a decongestant and cold and fever reducer—a sort of natural NyQuil—as well as for various other ailments.

Fast-forward several centuries, and you'll find that ephedrine, the active element in a host of drugs for treating asthma, nasal, and chest congestion, and other respiratory ills, is none other than the same element found in good old ephedra. Medicinal ephedrine,

---

A Word of Caution

Part of the fun in working with herbs is in learning their healthful qualities, both ancient and modern. But as an herbal businessperson, you must be very careful not to make promises. You can, for instance, sell starter plants of echinacea for the home gardener; sell harvested leaves to makers of herbal remedies, or package the leaves yourself to sell as a tea. But you cannot tell people that echinacea—or any other herb—will cure any sort of disease or malady.

The FDA strictly prohibits this type of activity. New laws are being discussed, and hopefully written, about herbal preparations, but for now they don't count as medicine in the eyes of the federal government. And making claims leaves your door wide open for all sorts of legal problems.

Remember that while you may be wise in the ways of herbs, you're not a doctor or any other sort of health-care practitioner, and you don't want customers to think of you as such. Offer suggestions as to what various herbs are traditionally used for, and give customers literature to read. Use caution and common sense, and as an extra precaution, consult a knowledgeable attorney before you set up shop.

like lots of pharmaceuticals, can be derived directly from the botanical source, or it can be synthetically reproduced in the laboratory.

It's far healthier, herbal proponents argue, to use botanical drugs as nature provided them rather than introduce synthetic materials into our bodies. Traditional scientists, on the other hand, insist that phytomedicinals are problematic because they're plants and therefore complex compounds. If you treat someone with ephedrine, you know you're giving him a single identifiable drug. But if you dose him with Mormon tea, you're also giving him a slew of other chemicals, the active characteristics of which may be unknown. And the debate rages on.

Farming in America

For centuries, America was a country of farmers. Most families lived on their own land, growing enough for themselves and hopefully enough extra to sell, or in towns and cities that were supplied by nearby farms. Even in urban areas, many people grew—as the colonists did—kitchen gardens that made it easy to stroll out the back door and pluck a few leaves of burnet for a salad, sage to season a stew, and mint to perk up the iced tea or julep. Dinner tables featured, as a matter of course, fresh herbs and vegetables that were either homegrown or came from fields only a few hours away. When the season ended, you canned what you could and waited until next year for the rest.

Full Steam Ahead

Then technology took a hand. Railroads crisscrossed the country, which meant that farmers could grow apples or tomatoes in New York and ship them to Montana or anywhere else in need of fresh produce. This was great in theory, but in practice, those rosy globes of good eating arrived at their destination more like mush than a firm meal.

So botanists developed cultivars, or cultivated varieties of fruits and vegetables capable of surviving cross-country travel. Iceberg lettuce, for instance, was designed to retain its shape and texture during shipping. And like many other specially bred cultivars, iceberg is a hardy traveler but doesn't taste like much of anything when compared to butter lettuces and other daintier varieties.

When produce suppliers discovered that they could keep fruits and vegetables "on ice" in refrigerated warehouses for months at a time, the fate of fresh food was sealed.

Cultivars were developed that not only traveled well but had about the same shelf life as plastic wrap. Store-bought produce came to bear only the faintest resemblance in taste—and sometimes even in looks—to the original product.

Back to the Farm

During World War II, the federal government began rationing food on the homefront so that as much as possible could be set aside for the soldiers. To compensate for the lack of meat, milk, and eggs, Americans grew victory gardens, which were really just old-fashioned kitchen gardens reborn. They learned to make vegetarian goodies like carrot and chickpea "burgers" and ate a lot of snap peas and green beans—and they felt good about doing their part for the war effort.

When the war ended and all those wonderful convenience foods hit the shelves, the victory gardens were plowed under to make room for rumpus rooms and swing sets. Small family farms gave way to huge conglomerates that used pesticides and other chemicals to step up production, and soon most people had no idea what real food from the garden tasted like—which meant that they also had no idea what fresh herbs tasted like. If it wasn't crushed or powdered and bottled in a little jar, it wasn't used.

In the 1960s and '70s, the garden clock began to turn back. Powered by flower children-types who wanted to get back to the land on their own small farm utopias, as well as media-fueled pesticide scares, Americans once more began producing real, organically grown food on real family farms. Encouraged by nouveau chefs like Alice Waters of the famed Chez Panisse restaurant in Berkeley, California, and home arts entrepreneurs like Martha Stewart, the market for specialty produce began to grow and then to thrive.

Today you can buy specialty market garden goodies—including, of course, herbs—at farmers' markets and green markets all over the country. Home shoppers and restaurant chefs alike look to local growers for farm-fresh products, just as they did long ago when the kitchen or market garden meant a victory for fine dining.

Culinary Delights

Even people who don't cook much more than spaghetti from a jar and cookies from the supermarket refrigerator case know that herbs and spices contribute mightily to the palatability of a meal. First off, fresh herbs impart flavors and textures quite unlike any dried, store-bought products you find. A scattering of fresh basil, sage, or oregano

Smart Tip

Herbs' essential oils are much more concentrated when the plant is dried, which means it takes less to flavor a dish. As a rule of thumb, use twice the amount of fresh herb in a recipe as you would dried.

Tip...

leaves make a ho-hum salad sing, while making the home or professional chef look like a genius. Fresh herbs in everything from soups and stews to breads and cookies impart a sparkle that enlivens even the dullest dinner. Rosemary stems used in place of wooden or metal skewers give grilled meats and vegetables a wonderfully romantic flavor. And candied violets or dainty rose petals dusted over desserts make a presentation fit for royalty.

Fun Fact

Coriander, a culinary and fragrance herb with a scent reminiscent of sage and citrus, was named for the bedbug because it presumably smells the same as the nasty pest.

Most people are aware that herbs can be used instead of salt to make any dish more interesting, as well as healthier. But wise cooks also know that certain herbs spike up foods' sweetness factor, helping them taste sweeter without adding sugar. Mint, bee balm, and costmary perk up iced beverages, lemon balm charges desserts, and rosemary adds zing to fruit-based dishes.

Cooking with herbs is exciting and presents incredibly diverse options. If you choose to specialize in culinary herbs, part of your mission will be to help your customers discover new herbs and new ways to use them. You can also develop your own line of culinary herb products—try some of the suggestions starting on page 24.

Scent-Sational Herbs

Herbs make an impact when used in the kitchen and medicine chest, but also as the base for bath and beauty products and home fragrances from potpourri and sachets to candles. The guiding idea behind all this is *aromatherapy*, the art and science of using botanical *essential oils*, or distilled plant essences, to stimulate the sense of smell and affect the rest of the body and the mind.

Aroma Sense

Fragrance reaches us through our olfactory organs, which are among the most powerful organs in the human body. According to the National Association for Holistic Aromatherapy (NAHA), when inhaled, essential oil molecules enter the nasal passages where they stimulate the olfactory nerve and send messages directly into the limbic area of the brain—the seat of memory, learning, and emotion. The inhalation of essential oil molecules causes physiological

Beware!

People who are pregnant, epileptic, or suffer chronic illnesses should consult a physician before using any essential oils.

Smart Tip

In aromatherapy circles, a synergy is a custom blend of various essential oils formulated for a specific purpose—for example, combining lemon oil (for uplifting spirits) and bergamot as an antidepressant.

changes within the body via the nervous, endocrine and immune systems; psychological changes also occur.

Scents entering the nose connect with the brain faster than just about any other stimuli at any other entry point of the body. Scientists have long proved that certain smells trigger powerful memories and associated emotions. The warm, homey scents of vanilla or cinnamon, for instance, make most people feel safe, secure, and relaxed as they conjure up memories of cookies—and love—from Mom's kitchen. Less obvious is that the scent of lavender helps to abolish insomnia and that rose oil is an antidepressant.

Essential oils can also be applied topically during massage or a bath or beauty treatment. Absorbed through the skin, they exert antibacterial, antifungal, anti-inflammatory, and psychological-lift properties. Add to this the fact that most essential oils just plain smell good, and you'll understand why aromatic herbal products are turning up all over the marketplace.

Princes and Elizabeths

Go one on one with Elizabeth Taylor, Elizabeth Arden, Prince Matchabelli, and Ralph Lauren to create your own line of fine fragrances. The art of making perfumes is an ancient one but also lots of fun. Start by consulting a few herb crafting and aromatherapy books for fragrance recipes. You might start with *Health and Beauty the Natural Way* (Metro Books), by Nerys Purchon, or *The Illustrated Encyclopedia of Herbs* (Rodale Press), which contain excellent sections on crafting herbal scents.

Like music, fragrances are composed of various notes, or types of scents—top, middle, and base notes. Just as you wouldn't want a symphony to be all high, reedy flutes and piccolos, you don't want to create a perfume that's all airy top notes. The art is in combining them with strong, rich base notes, as well as middle notes that add mellowness and depth.

You might, for instance, combine the sturdy base note of sandalwood with a top note of bergamot and a middle note of rose to create a mysterious, Near Eastern fragrance that would lift the spirits (bergamot and rose are antidepressants), as well as calm the mind (sandalwood is grounding). Take a look at the chart on opposite page for some ideas for your own blends.

Making Melodies with Herbal Notes

Essential Oil	Top	Middle	Base	Properties
Basil	✔			Invigorating and uplifting
Bergamot	✔			Refreshing, citrusy, antidepressant
Chamomile		✔		Fresh, soothing, and apple-scented
Clary sage		✔		Sweet, soothing, and floral
Eucalyptus	✔			Clean and bracing
Frankincense		✔		Smoky, spicy, and sweet
Grapefruit	✔			Refreshing and uplifting
Lavender		✔		Relaxing and soothing
Lemon	✔			Fresh and invigorating
Neroli		✔		Another name for orange blossom—sweet, feminine, and soothing
Patchouli			✔	Spicy and earthy
Peppermint	✔			Refreshing and stimulating
Pine			✔	Fresh, clean, and masculine
Rose		✔		Romantic and an antidepressant
Rosemary		✔		Energizing and refreshing
Sandalwood			✔	Woodsy, calming, grounding, and masculine
Thyme		✔		Warm and sweet
Ylang-ylang			✔	Exotic, floral, and an aphrodisiac

Nothing Like the Real Thing

You should note that true essential oils are expensive because of the amount of raw product necessary to make them. A single pound of authentic, unadulterated rose oil, for instance, requires about 2,000 pounds of rose petals. The petals—or other raw botanicals—are usually processed through *steam distillation*, which, in a sort of twist on the moonshine production of yore, uses a still to vaporize and condense the herb's natural oils that are then separated from the remaining water. Many essential oils on the market are at least partially synthetic; industry experts generally insist that they're inferior and won't provide therapeutic effects.

Beware!

Most essential oils are too strong to be used directly on the skin and can irritate. If used for massages or other direct applications, however, essential oils should be mixed with carrier oils like avocado, jojoba, or other vegetable-, nut-, or seed-based products—which have the added bonus of being skin-nutritive.

How do you know which is the real thing? There are several ways:

- *Cost.* Compare prices of various brands. The more inexpensive an oil, the more likely it is to be synthetic.
- *Labeling.* If the label says "fragrance," you can assume it's derived from petroleum and thus not a natural plant essence.
- *Feel.* Unadulterated essential oils are actually more the consistency of water than oil. If the product you're examining feels greasy, it most likely has been mixed with a carrier oil—a vegetable, nut, or seed oil like good old kitchen olive oil or almond oil.

NAHA is working toward legislation that would require true essential oils to be labeled with a TAP, or *true aromatherapy product*, designation as well as their Latin names, like *lavendula vera* for lavender.

Putting It Together

As an herbal entrepreneur, you may decide to craft your own private-label herbal products. Or you may choose to grow the herbs but let your customers do the stillroom stuff. Either way, you'll need to know a tincture from a tea from an infusion. Keep in mind that the following are general descriptions, not actual recipes. You must follow recipes from reputable sources before making any herbal product either for yourself or for sale.

Taking Tea

- *Tea.* This is the preparation most people are familiar with, made by steeping leaves, flowers, or stems in boiled water. Medicinal teas tend to be much stronger than the "cuppa," as the Brits say, that's brewed for the pleasure of an afternoon—or anytime—sip.

- *Tisane.* Depending on who you're talking to, this can be either a very strong tea, made by using a greater quantity of herbs per cup than you'd use for a regular cuppa, or just a fancy word for tea.

- *Infusion.* This is another term for tea, but may also refer to a tea that's steeped for as long as several hours. An infusion can also be added to bath water for a whole-body experience.

- *Decoction.* This extract is made with sturdy raw ingredients like roots and bark that demand more steeping time. Typically, decoctions are simmered for up to an hour, whereas teas never simmer and are steeped for only a few minutes.

- *Tincture.* This potent extract is made by steeping an herb or herb blend in drinkable spirits like brandy, gin, or vodka (never, ever rubbing alcohol or any other nonpotable spirit) for as long as six weeks. The resulting concentrate is then taken in drop-sized doses mixed with water or juice.

- *Syrup.* Syrups are made by combining herbal infusions or decoctions with honey.

- *Herbal vinegar.* This culinary vinegar is made by steeping fresh herbs in vinegar for up to six weeks. Herb vinegars can also be used as facial or hair conditioners. The word "vinegar" comes from the French words *vin aigre*, which means "sour wine," a handy reminder that experts suggest cider vinegar from apples or wine vinegars are too harsh for body preparations.

- *Herbal culinary oil.* This is similar to herbal vinegar, but made with quality cooking oil.

- *Bouquet garni.* Basically a tea bag for the cook pot, this is a pastiche of herbs tied up in a cheesecloth bag or sometimes a bundle of herb sprigs bound with string. The herbs infuse the food as you cook without leaving leaves, twigs, or other unpalatable bits for unwary diners.

Beauty and the Bath

Making your own brand of bath and beauty products is easier than you might imagine. It's also lots of fun! Just take care, as with teas, tisanes, and other culinary products, to follow directions carefully, not only for preparation but for storage. We've listed some of the basics here, but there are lots more—start researching and choose the ones you want to make (and, of course, that you believe will sell).

- *Infused oil.* Not to be confused with a culinary oil, this is also made by steeping fresh herbs in oil.

- *Salve or ointment.* This is made by mixing infused oil with beeswax.
- *Herb water.* This infusion for external use is made from fresh herbs steeped in water or from water mixed with essential oil.
- *Lotion.* A lotion can consist of anything from a bracing herb water to be splashed on the skin to mixtures

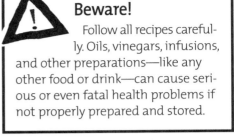

Beware!
Follow all recipes carefully. Oils, vinegars, infusions, and other preparations—like any other food or drink—can cause serious or even fatal health problems if not properly prepared and stored.

including various combinations of lanolin, beeswax, vegetable oils, or glycerin and essential oils.

- *Soap.* Soaps can be hand-milled, made from a premade soap base that's grated and combined with essential oils and other ingredients like lanolin, herb water or wheat germ, then molded into bars, balls, or fun shapes from stars to fish. This method is also called melt-and-pour. Soap can also be made by cold process or hot process, which are old-fashioned, from-scratch methods involving sodium hydroxide, which is basically lye.
- *Shampoo.* This can be made from scratch with finely grated pure soap, water, borax, and essential oils. Or you can make a quickie version using baby shampoo as a base, then adding essential oils and other ingredients.
- *Bath bag.* This is simply tea for the bath—a muslin or cheesecloth bag stuffed with fresh or dried herbs and sometimes oatmeal or instant milk powder (like Cleopatra's famous milk bath).
- *Perfume, cologne, and toilet water.* These are all variations on the theme of personal fragrance, the only real difference being the ratio of essential oils to other ingredients. Perfumes are the strongest (which is why they're the most expensive at your favorite cosmetics counter), with colognes coming in second and toilet waters containing the weakest concentration of oils. In addition to essential oils, personal fragrances typically contain alcohol like vodka, water, and glycerin.

On the Homefront

As long as you're designing your own line of teas and tisanes or bath and beauty products, why not develop a line of home care and décor products to match? It's easy, fun, and adds to your bottom line. Try these ideas for starters:

- *Potpourri.* Just about everybody recognizes potpourri these days, and it's still extremely popular. Pronounced POH-poor-ee, this is a mixture of dried botanicals from flower petals and leaves to bits of bark, seed pods, citrus peels, and even dried fruit slices made more fragrant with the addition of essential oils. Some potpourri recipes call for the addition of a fixative, usually botanicals like orris root, vetiver root, or benzoin.

- *Sachet.* This is a delightful product from Grandma's era and earlier—it includes the same ingredients as potpourri, but they are ground or crumbled and sewn into dainty fabric bags. Sachets are tucked into lingerie and clothing drawers, stashed in linen cupboards, hidden behind living room sofa cushions, and popped into used or unused suitcases to banish the musty smell.

- *Sleep or dream pillow.* Another version of the sachet, the dream pillow is a fabric pocket filled with dried herbs that promote restful sleep and pleasant dreams. You might also design a special sleep pal for children—a teddy bear, bunny, or other stuffed toy filled with aromatic and safe, sleep-inducing herbs.

- *Pomander ball.* A traditional Christmas gift that can be used—and sold—at any time of the year, the pomander ball is an orange, lime, or other citrus fruit liberally studded with cloves. Some recipes call for the ball to be dusted with cinnamon, nutmeg, and other cookie spices which are mixed with orris root as a fixative. You can then wrap pomander balls in ribbon and suspend them from clothes-closet rods or mound them in a bowl for a delightfully different sort of potpourri.

- *Room spray, mist, or refresher.* This is the herbal version of those store-bought room deodorizers without all the additives—or the peculiar after-odor. Room sprays can be used to set a mood, to aid in cleansing airborne germs or simply to perfume a living or work space. They typically consist of essential oils mixed with alcohol and purified water and dispensed in a spray bottle.

- *Candle.* Herb-scented candles have been around for centuries—one example that everyone is familiar with is the colonists' bayberry tapers. Make your own by mixing essential oils, powdered herbs or fresh botanicals into wax before forming in molds.

- *Wreath.* A staple of the herbal business, wreaths are eternally popular. Besides the conventional product crafted with dried botanicals, you can also make living wreaths, as well as other shapes—from herbs planted in sphagnum moss-covered chicken wire forms.

- *Fairy house.* Once relegated to the pages of children's classics, fairies are enjoying new popularity, with flower fairy cards, books, figurines, and other merchandise popping up everywhere you look. Fairy houses are tiny dwellings crafted of twigs, moss, bark, seed pods, and other botanicals carefully glued onto cardboard frames.

- *Herb basket.* Cover or line a simple basket with moss and dried or living botanicals, fill it with more herbs, and you've got yourself an herb basket.

> **Bright Idea**
> Add a few teaspoons of an herbal infusion to a bottle of ink to create herbal-scented ink. You might sell lavender ink along with pressed-lavender note cards, romantic neroli ink with Valentine's greetings, or balsam or pine ink with Christmas cards.

- *Tussie-mussie or nosegay.* This is a bouquet that carries a message in herbs and flowers. In Victorian times, botanicals had not only scents but specific meanings; if you gave someone a violet, for example, it meant you were devoted, while bee balm spoke of virtue and borage of bravery. For more on the meanings of various flowers, see "The Language of Flowers" on page 30.

> **Fun Fact**
> You'll find caffeine, the active ingredient in coffee—an herb not commonly grown in the continental United States—listed as a basic ingredient in both prescription and over-the-counter headache remedies, even some aspirins.

Where the Wild Things Are

Most herbal entrepreneurs grow their own botanicals, purchase them from wholesalers or other growers, or some combination thereof. But some intrepid souls garner their herbs through wildcrafting, which is another way of saying foraging.

Many of the plants we recognize as herbs are really domesticated weeds and still grow wild in fields, forests, and roadsides all over this country and all around the globe. A weekend tramp through the outdoors foraging for these wild gems can be a fun, invigorating, and inexpensive way to supplement your herbal stores and increase your income while exercising your body and communing with nature.

A Cautionary Tale

Like other aspects of the herb industry, wildcrafting has its detractors. One reason is that herb hunting can be dangerous. If you don't really know your plants, you could easily mistake a poisonous herb for an innocuous one. Industry experts often cite the tale of an older lady who decided to dose herself and her husband with tea made from foraged comfrey leaves as a remedy for their arthritis. Unfortunately, what she brewed turned out to be toxic foxglove—which looks similar—and the couple died within hours.

And even if you can tell dandelion from digitalis with absolute certainty, you may not know whether plants foraged from fields or roadsides have been doused with pesticides, car exhaust fumes, or other toxic substances.

Opponents of wildcrafting also complain that plucking plants indiscriminately from their native habitats contributes to their extinction. Not so, say responsible wildcraft enthusiasts. They argue that picking some

> **Beware!**
> In some areas, especially government lands, you need a permit to forage. Always ask before you wildcraft, not only on public but also on private properties.

Pretty Poison

While herbs can be a healthy alternative to OTC (over-the-counter) and prescription drugs or bath, beauty, and home-care products, they can also be dangerous. Like all botanicals, some are outright poisonous. Deadly nightshade, aconite, and hemlock are herbs commonly recognized as poisonous, but licorice, lobelia, goldenseal, and even aloe—touted as a cure-all for minor cuts and burns—are also toxic when ingested. Some essential oils and herbs, including myrrh, peppermint, and rosemary oils, as well as the homely parsley plant, can be dangerous for pregnant women. Various herbs can cause kidney or liver damage when used improperly. And even that herbal remedy poster plant, St. John's wort, can cause photosensitivity, an oversensitivity to sunlight.

Even herbs that are generally recognized as safe can be toxic when overused; don't make the mistake of thinking that if two drops of tincture are good, four, 10, or 12 must be better. What's true of coffee, champagne, and most of life's pleasures is also true for herbs—moderation is the key.

And as always with all things herbal: Do your homework, and if you don't know, ask an expert.

botanicals, like the invasive kudzu of the South that grows as much as 2 feet per day in summer and chokes out native plants, is actually a boon to property owners and natural species. Responsible wildcrafters, like Johnny Appleseed, also replant as they go, scattering seeds or planting roots and crowns. Another option is to form a partnership with an organic farmer to harvest weeds he views as pests but which are useful to the herbal entrepreneur.

The keys to wildcrafting are knowledge and responsibility. You must be able to recognize safe plants and chemically safe habitats. You should respect the planet by picking only botanicals that are either non-native and invasive or abound in a wide region. Replant as you go, leave plenty of mother plants to reproduce, don't take more than you need, and have fun. That's important, too!

Fun Fact

People are often confused about the difference between herbs and spices. Although there is no clear-cut answer, experts generally agree that spices are the seeds, bark, or other parts of tropical plants (think cinnamon and nutmeg), while herbs are the leaves or other parts of temperate climate plants, like lavender and basil.

The Language of Flowers

Herb	Meaning	Possible Use
Aloe	Healing	To heal a lover's quarrel or as a get-well wish
Angelica	Inspiration	For romance; "you inspire me"; or as a wish for a creative friend
Basil	Love, warm wishes—or conversely, hate	For romance—forget the hate part
Bay	Accomplishment, victory, and fame	For a graduation, a promotion, or an athletic or creative win
Bee balm	Virtue	To celebrate the virtue of a parent or care-giver
Borage	Bravery	For bravery in overcoming any number of modern challenges
Chamomile	Wisdom	For a favorite teacher or mentor
Dill	Survival and good cheer	For get-well wishes
Geranium, scented	Happiness	For a new baby
Goldenrod	Encouragement	For get-well wishes, to encourage a romance, or success in a difficult effort
Lady's mantle	Protection	For a new baby
Lavender	Devotion	For romance or as thanks to a parent or care-giver
Marjoram	Joy	For romance or a new baby
Parsley	Merriment	For romance or a new baby
Rose	Love and success	For romance or success in a venture
Rosemary	Remembrance	For condolences, an anniversary, or a reunion
Sage	Health and longevity	For get-well wishes or a birthday
Thyme	Daring	For success in a venture
Violet	Modesty or devotion	For romance

Herbs 101
How to Tell Bee Balm from Basil

With more than 10,000 herbs in the world, even the most pre-eminent herbalist would be hard-pressed to know, or even recognize, them all. But there are dozens that are considered common, and they're the ones with which you'll want to be on familiar terms.

Herbs have an incredibly rich and varied history, folklore, and multitude of uses, whether medicinal, cosmetic or culinary. The more you read, and research, the more there is to learn—and the more fascinated you become.

We could devote pages to each herb, but since this is a business guide rather than an herb encyclopedia, we've chosen instead to present a brief portrait—really a sketch—of each plant. Keep in mind that there may be many more medicinal, culinary, cosmetic, or other uses (such as fabric dyes, crafts, or companion planting) than those we've touched on here. Keep in mind, too, that it's up to you to research these applications and determine their validity—especially when it comes to health matters.

Photo© PhotoDisc Inc.

The Portrait Gallery

- *Angelica.* A stately herb that can reach 8 feet in height, angelica has a sweet, licorice-like taste that makes it a hit in the kitchen—as well as the liquor cabinet. It's one of the ingredients that give Benedictine and Chartreuse their unique flavors. Angelica has traditionally been used medicinally for both digestive and respiratory problems, but modern herbalists feel that it may be unsafe when used as a health remedy. The herb's essential oil makes angelically scented bath and beauty products.

- *Basil.* Perennially popular, basil is traditionally used to flavor Italian dishes but also stars in Thai and other Mediterranean meals. With a taste reminiscent of cloves and mint, it's sometimes used in after-dinner tea to aid in digestion, as well as a remedy for depression and nausea. Basil's refreshing fragrance makes it shine in bath and beauty products. Gardeners have long prized the herb as a companion to tomatoes; it repels insects and contributes to growth.

- *Bay.* The leaves of the bay tree find a home in nearly every kitchen—they're traditionally used in soups, stews, and sauces, as well as in pickling. Bay is also used as a topical remedy for aching joints and muscles, and as a skin lotion, although some people suffer an allergic reaction to it. The herb is also used to repel weevils and other bugs in cereals and grains.

- *Bee balm.* Also known as Oswego tea for the Oswego (or, more correctly, Otsego) Indians who introduced it to American colonists, this crimson-flowered shrub can reach 6 feet in height. In addition to a brew for tea, citrusy bee balm leaves can be used to flavor fruit and salad dishes, as well as a variety of meat entrees. The flowers make a fine garnish for fancying up foods and attract not only humans but also bees, butterflies, and hummingbirds. Bee balm is also called bergamot because its aroma is similar to that of the oil of orange bergamot, a tropical tree. Bee balm's essential oil is used to scent potpourri and sachets, as well as bath and beauty products.

> **Fun Fact**
> Angelica was once worn in strands around children's necks as a protection against disease.

- *Calendula.* With its sunny yellow flowers, calendula shines as an ornamental in the garden and, after drying, as a cheerful addition to wreaths, potpourri, and other crafts. As a herbal remedy, calendula—also called pot marigold—is traditionally used to treat bruises, burns, and rashes and to help heal wounds, as well as canker sores and menstrual distress. In the kitchen, calendula petals can be tossed in salads, used as a garnish, or ground and substituted for expensive saffron. And in the bath, calendula is commonly used in rinses for blonde and brunette hair.

- *Catnip.* Related to mint, this weedy perennial has been a favorite among cats and their people for eons. Because felines find catnip's scent intoxicating, it makes an ideal ingredient in any number of stuffed and sewn cat toys. For humans, the lemony, minty herb is used as a digestive aid and mild sedative when steeped as a tea and can also add zing to salads. Some herbalists recommend caution to pregnant women.

- *Chamomile.* Chamomile tea has long been known for its soporific effects—Peter Rabbit's mum gave it to him after a traumatic day in Mr. MacGregor's garden. Because the tea is brewed from flowers and contains their pollens, some people may suffer allergic reactions to it. Medicinally, the oil from these miniature daisy lookalikes is known as a mild sedative, anxiety reducer, and sleep promoter, as well as an anti-inflammatory and anti-spasmodic. Chamomile's soft, apple fragrance makes it a standout in potpourri and sachets. Infusions of chamomile make terrific rinses for bringing out the highlights in blondes and brunettes. In the garden, chamomile is praised as a companion to cucumbers, onions, most other herbs and indeed most plants. And chamomile

> **Fun Fact**
> Dandelion gets its name from the French *dent de lion,* or lion's tooth, a description of its notched leaves.

also makes a fragrant ground cover that springs back after being trampled while it releases its signature scent.

- *Dandelion.* You thought it was only a lowly weed, but yes, it's really an herb. Medicinally, dandelion is used as a mild diuretic and laxative and in Europe is also known as a remedy for

Beware!
Pennyroyal, a member of the mint family, makes a potent insect repellent but is also quite toxic. Don't confuse it with other milder mints.

anemia, diabetes, and liver diseases. In the kitchen, dandelion is newly trendy in wine, salads with other wild greens, or cooked like spinach or collards. The crayon yellow flowers can be used as garnishes and to add sunshine shades to butters, spreads, and vinegars. Roasted dandelion roots are used—like chicory—in place of coffee. And dandelions are used to make yellow and magenta dyes for wool.

- *Dill.* Anyone who's eaten a pickle has tasted dill. But most people don't realize that the feathery plant is also used by herbalists to step up production of mother's milk, calm colicky babies, stimulate appetites, and settle upset tummies. In the kitchen, of course, aside from pickling, the piquant dill is used as a seasoning for fish, lamb, eggs, and vegetables. In the garden, dill is said to aid in the cultivation of lettuces, cabbages, and onions. And dried dill foliage and flowers make airy additions to wreaths and other dried botanical projects.

- *Echinacea.* Also known by its common name, purple coneflower, this wildflower is one of the biggest media stars on the herbal remedy scene. Herbalists tout its antibiotic and blood-cleansing properties. In the garden, echinacea is a delightful ornamental that can come indoors as part of a cut-flower bouquet or be left alone outdoors to spread into a purple profusion of blooms.

- *Fennel.* Like dill, fennel is an airy herb with feathery flowers on slender stalks. Like angelica, it has a distinct licorice-like flavor and fragrance. Medicinally, fennel is said to aid digestion, relieve colicky babies (and their parents), and increase milk flow in nursing moms. In the kitchen, fennel seeds flavor desserts and baked goods, leaves and stems show up in salads, and fennel oil adds intrigue to liqueurs. In the bath, the essential oil is used for soaps, creams and perfumes. Take care—fennel oil can be dangerous for people with sensitive skin or allergies.

- *Garlic.* The bane of vampires, garlic is not just a kitchen staple for making pungent dishes but also an herb with healing qualities. Garlic boasts powerful antibacterial powers and has been shown to take action against staph and strep bacteria, some flu viruses, and even yeast infections like athlete's foot. Garlic's healing properties are more effective when consumed raw. And according to some herbalists, it should not be fed to small children. In the kitchen, garlic can be used in just about every dish imaginable except sweets—although there is a garlic ice cream out there. In the garden, garlic makes a terrific companion plant that keeps aphids from munching on roses.

- *Lavender.* Although freely used by the ancient Greeks and Romans, until our current herbal renaissance lavender was basically considered a fragrance for dear old ladies. Today, however, lavender's clean, fresh scent infuses bath and beauty products galore, including sachets, potpourri, perfumes, and candles. Medicinally, lavender is an antidepressant that also reduces fatigue and relieves headaches, but, like all herbal remedies, it should be used in moderation. It is also used to treat skin conditions like eczema, as well as bruises and bites. In the kitchen, the fragrant flowers and leaves are used as garnishes and in salads, candies, vinegars, and even jellies. In housekeeping, lavender is used in furniture polish and as an antiviral and antiseptic room spray.

- *Lemon balm.* A member of the mint family, lemon balm is used to unstop a stuffy nose, soothe the nerves, and aid in digestion, and is also said to help lower blood pressure. In the kitchen, it adds a subtle melody of lemon and mint to salads and fruits, as well as poultry and fish dishes. In the bath, lemon balm is used as a skin cleanser and as a steam treatment for acne. In the garden, the yellow-green plant attracts bees but repels other insects. And in the house, lemon balm can be used as lemon-scented furniture polish—an herbal, environmentally safe alternative to commercially made polishes.

- *Lovage.* A standard of the medieval kitchen and physick gardens, lovage tastes similar to celery but is easier to grow. As a remedy, lovage has diuretic properties and works to relieve flatulence. In the kitchen, it can be used in salads, soups, stews, spreads and sauces, and in pickling.

- *Marjoram.* The Greeks called marjoram "joy of the mountains," and whether you grow it in the Rockies or the Great Plains, you'll agree. Medicinally, this Mediterranean herb is used to relieve headaches, sinus congestion, and minor coughs, but should not be used during pregnancy or menstruation. In the kitchen, its oregano-like flavor is a terrific seasoning for any dish in which you'd use garlic, thyme, and basil. In housekeeping, marjoram is often used to freshen linen closets and chests, as an ingredient in potpourri and sachets, and as a furniture polish. Dried sprigs of the fragrant herb also make wonderful additions to wreaths and other botanical crafts.

- *Mint.* Refreshing mint is beloved by imbibers of iced teas and mint juleps,

Fun Fact

The ancient Romans wore parsley wreaths or necklaces during orgies in the belief that the herb would absorb alcohol fumes so they could continue to drink without getting drunk.

sticky-fingered slurpers of candy canes, and makers of mouthwashes and toothpastes, not to mention cooks worldwide. Medicinally, mint contains menthol, a digestive aid and an antispasmodic, which relieves upset stomachs and menstrual cramping. Mint is also used as a remedy for flatulence and nausea; in aromatherapy, it's used to invigorate and energize. Of the nearly dozen varieties of mint available to gardeners, peppermint seems to be the one with the most medicinal effects (use with caution for infants and small children). In the kitchen, mint lends itself to virtually any sweet or savory dish or beverage. In the bath, mint makes an invigorating cleanser and fragrance and is said to control dandruff. Mint adds sparkle to sachets and potpourri while repelling mice, and in the garden, mint is said to banish aphids and other plant pests.

- *Nasturtium.* Sunny nasturtium flowers in hues of yellows and oranges make cheerful denizens of the garden, as well as the kitchen. Nasturtiums' peppery, pungent flowers add pizzazz to salads and sandwiches and make festive food garnishes. In the garden, nasturtium has long been known as an easy-grow com-

What's in a Name?

While many people have both formal names—their first, middle and surnames—as well as nicknames, all plants have both scientific (or formal) names and common names. Common names can be confusing; the same plant can be known by a half dozen different monikers in different parts of the country, let alone the world. Bee balm, for example, is also called Oswego tea and bergamot in North America, while in Europe it goes by the names golden Melissa and Indian nettle. And to confuse things further, bergamot is also the common name of orange bergamot, a tropical tree.

But take heart. Bee balm's scientific name, *Monarda didyma*, instantly identifies it as the mint-related plant known to the American Indians and not tropical Citrus bergamia, the tree.

You should also note that many herbs come in several varieties. You'll find, for instance, spearmint or *Mentha spicata*, apple mint or *Mentha suaveolens*, and bergamot mint or *Mentha Xpiperita varcitrata*, among many others. And some botanicals, like chamomile, while often referred to as a single herb, can actually be either one of two entirely different plants: *Chamaemelum nobile*, or Roman chamomile, and *Matricaria chamomilla*, or German chamomile.

With all these possibilities for confusion, you'll want to familiarize yourself with the scientific names and make sure the botanical you've chosen is the right one for your intended application.

panion plant that reputedly repels whiteflies and other plant nasties.

- *Oregano.* Closely related to marjoram, oregano is its brasher cousin, with a stronger fragrance and flavor. Oregano is a staple in pizza and spaghetti sauces and other Italian dishes, but also stars

Smart Tip — Tip...

Herbs make good house-plants. Among the stars of the kitchen windowsill are basil, chives, dill, marjoram, and the mints.

in Greek, Mexican, Spanish, Cuban, and Brazilian cooking, to name just a few. As an herbal remedy, oregano is said to aid in digestion, as well as to relieve colic, motion sickness, and even toothaches. As a seasoning, the Mediterranean native stars in the same dishes as marjoram, and the fresh leaves are a lively addition to salads. On the craft front, sprigs of oregano perk up dried botanical wreaths and can also make stellar additions to culinary wreaths made from fresh herbs.

- *Parsley.* Considered by most people as a staple garnish on restaurant plates but not particularly edible, parsley is actually packed with healthy properties. It boasts vitamins A and C, several B vitamins, calcium, and iron. Medicinally, parsley has diuretic and laxative properties, relieves indigestion, and is an excellent after-dinner breath freshener. Parsley should not be used during pregnancy. In the kitchen, this bright green herb does indeed make a nice plate garnish, but is also used as a seasoning. In the bath, parsley's essential oil is an ingredient in perfumes, soaps and shampoos.

- *Rose.* A plea for forgiveness from errant spouses, a symbol of devotion delivered to Mom on Mother's Day, or a splashy declaration of passion, roses are emblems of love the world over. They're also potent herbs. Like parsley, rose hips (the flower's "fruit") contain more vitamin C per ounce than an orange. They're also packed with vitamins A, B, E, and K, while rose petals have an astringent property. Medicinally, roses are used to soothe sore throats and stave off colds. In the kitchen, the rose's inherent pectin makes it a terrific base for jams, jellies, and conserves. A garnish of fresh rose petals, either *au naturel* or candied, turns any dessert into a showpiece. In the bath, rose petals can be used in skin lotions and cleansers. And of course *attar of roses*, the proper term for rose oil, adds an intoxicating fragrance to any perfume or beauty product. On the home front, the rose is perhaps the most popular ingredient in potpourri and sachets, as well as in wreaths and other botanical crafts.

- *Rosemary.* If you know your Shakespeare, you know that "rosemary is for remembrance," as the doomed Ophelia in Hamlet says. But while this gray-green Mediterranean herb does mean remembrance in the language of herbs, it means much more in culinary and herb medicine circles. As a remedy, pungent, pine-scented rosemary is said to relieve flatulence, headaches, and depression. In the kitchen, rosemary brightens just about any dish except sweets. In the bath, rosemary shines in any number of shampoos, hair rinses (for brunettes), soaps, and perfumes. In housekeeping, its bold scent enlivens sachets and potpourris.

- *Sage.* Most people tend to think of silvery-green sage merely as a seasoning for Thanksgiving turkey and stuffing. But there's much more to this herb than just once-a-year flavoring. Medicinally, sage is used as a remedy for sore throats, canker sores, and other mouth irritations. In the kitchen, the outdoorsy, faintly lemony flavor of its leaves does wonders when used fresh in salads or cooked in a wide variety of meat and vegetable dishes and baked goods. In the bath, sage is sometimes used as an antiperspirant, as well as an ingredient in soaps, skin lotions, and fragrances. In housekeeping, sage leaves make interesting additions to potpourri, sachets, and dried botanicals. In the garden, sage repels pests while attracting bees.

- *Savory.* While not particularly well-known today, savory herbs were popular culinary seasonings during the last two millennia. There are actually two different savories: summer and winter. The latter is more pungent, with a piney flavor, while summer savory lends a peppery essence to foods. In the kitchen, summer savory perks up beans and other vegetables, as well as chicken and fish dishes. Winter savory is more often used with stronger meats, including wild game.

- *Scented geranium.* A native of South Africa, the scented geranium—which is not really a geranium but a pelargonium—counts as a delightfully fragrant herb. In the kitchen, the leaves of this Victorian favorite are used to brew delicately scented teas, infuse cakes and sugars, and garnish salads and desserts. In the bath and home, the many species of scented geranium, including rose, mint, cinnamon, lemon, and apple, add signature fragrances to perfumes and other bath and beauty products, as well as sachets and potpourri.

- *St. John's wort.* Another poster plant in the new renaissance of herbs, St. John's wort is widely touted as a remedy for depression and anxiety but is also used to treat wounds, burns, cuts, ulcers, and even injured nerve tissues. The yellow-flowered herb, however, has also been found to cause photosensitivity, or sensitivity to sunlight, so it should be used medicinally with caution or not at all. St. John's wort makes a sunny addition to the garden and is easy to grow.

- *Tarragon.* This versatile culinary herb is a staple ingredient of many popular kitchen products, including tartar and béarnaise sauces and French dressing. Slender tarragon bolsters fish, meats, poultry, and vegetables, and makes a flavorful herb vinegar. In the bath, tarragon's pungent licorice-like fragrance enlivens soaps, perfumes, and other fragrances. And in the garden, the Siberian native makes a sturdy companion to most vegetables by encouraging growth.

- *Thyme.* With its tiny leaves, thyme may look timid, but it's one of the most powerful herbs in both the kitchen and physick garden. The essential oil of this Mediterranean native contains thymol, which is used in many commercially prepared mouthwashes and toothpastes. Medicinally, thyme's antiseptic and apparent antispasmodic properties are used to treat respiratory problems, tummy and headaches, sore throats, and coughs. Thyme's potency indicates caution; its essential oil should not be ingested in pure form, and some people can suffer allergic reactions when it's used even indirectly on the skin. In the kitchen, thyme lends its unique aroma to Greek, French, Creole, and Cajun foods, as well as just about any other meat or vegetable dish. In the bath, thyme is used as an ingredient in fragrances, soaps, and lotions. In housekeeping, a thyme room spray or infusion can be used as a disinfectant, while thyme sprigs or sachets keep bugs out of linens and clothing. In the garden, thyme is a timely companion to tomatoes, potatoes, and eggplants and repels whiteflies while attracting bees. Like chamomile, it also makes a charming ground cover that releases its aroma when stepped on or brushed against, yet resists trampling.

4

A
Well-Designed
Garden
Market Research

Every good garden and farm is carefully designed with plots, beds, and crops laid out to take advantage of the soil, climate, seasons, and weather. You'll want to artfully design your herb business in the same manner, planning what you'll grow, who you'll sell those crops to and how you'll promote them. In other words, you'll want to conduct market research.

This is an extremely important part of any new business start-up. The more facts and figures you plant in your head, the more information about your potential customers you sow, the greater rewards you'll reap. Market research helps you determine not only if there are enough customers in your area for the types of herbs you want to grow but even what sorts of herbs those potential customers would want to buy. By the time you're ready to throw open your garden gate for business, you'll know all about your customer base.

Target Your Market

First, you'll want to decide exactly what type of herb business you'll run and who your customers will be. You've got a lot of options to choose from, and you don't have to relegate yourself to just one model—lots of successful herbal entrepreneurs mix and match operations. Get creative, and find an option that suits both you and your target market.

Wholesale Alternative

You don't need to limit your options to business-to-business customers, selling directly to chefs, markets, and garden centers; you can also sell to wholesalers and distributors. These are companies who buy up great truckloads of fresh-cut or potted herbs from growers, then turn around and sell them to (you guessed it) chefs, markets, and garden centers—but they also sell a lot of herbs to other herb growers. Why? Growers who don't have greenhouses often purchase herbs from wholesalers so they can continue selling out of their season or when they need more stock than they have available for a particular order.

Wholesalers sell herbs not only to restaurants, markets, and garden centers, but also to the health-products industry for use in vitamins and supplements, to the cosmetic industry for use in hair- and skin-care products, to herbal tea producers and food manufacturers, and to crafts stores.

Selling to wholesalers isn't as much fun as selling directly to your customers. You don't get the interaction and feedback or the rush of seeing people enjoy the rewards of your labors. But if you're just not a people person, this can be a good alternative.

There's no rule that says you have to sell strictly wholesale or retail. Mix and match your customers, so long as it fits your market niche. "I sell both wholesale and retail," says herb grower and Texas Herb Growers and Marketers Association vice president Cindy M. in Hallettsville, Texas. "I started out mainly selling wholesale, but since I enjoy customer contact, I decided to sell retail as well. My wholesale customers are mostly retail nurseries in the larger towns within about a 100-mile radius. Retail customers are mostly local people looking for something different that the larger, more general nurseries don't sell. Also, people of different ethnic backgrounds look for herbs to cook with that they can't find in the grocery stores locally. I also sell at local festivals, market days, and farmers' markets in the area."

Michele B. in Soddy Daisy, Tennessee, on the other hand, finds her best market is retail mail order. "My customer base is anyone from the novice gardener to retirees, crafters, soap makers, and even those folks who are looking for something different to give as gifts, like for Bosses Day or a Thanksgiving basket of herbs," she says. "We also have been asked to do gift certificates."

A Cut Above

Perhaps the easiest and least expensive way to get started is to sell fresh-cut herbs to restaurants and grocers. You grow the herbs they want, then harvest and deliver them as needed, usually once or twice a week.

Trendy eateries can be a terrific market for your products. Chefs don't have to be convinced of the difference fresh herbs can make in a meal and can be eager buyers. They're generally interested in the usual cast of characters from the herbal garden, from basil and cilantro to dill and mint, but they can also be excellent experimenters. If you suggest something new, be it epazote, sorrel, or summer savory, a chef will be more likely to try it than a supermarket manager.

The specialty market also makes a great customer. This is not the supermarket or the corner convenience store that stocks your basic white bread and bologna, but the upscale shop that showcases fresh breads and pastries, fine wines, 15 different kinds of olives, 40 kinds of cheeses, and fashionable produce like baby squash and heirloom tomatoes. This is where you come in, because herbs are also chic. Specialty grocers may not be as experimental-minded as their great chef counterparts, but they're good customers of all the usual herbs plus any making food-trend headlines.

And don't overlook natural-food stores. You know the ones—the grocery markets suspended in time (somewhere in the 1970s) that carry the really healthy stuff like stone-ground wheat, industrial-strength bran, strangely chewy power bars instead of candy, cookies made with fruit juice instead of sugar, and strictly organic produce. These stores are also terrific customers for pesticide-free fresh herbs—like yours!

Supermarkets provide a market for the herb grower, but they're not necessarily your best bet. Yes, most chain grocery stores, from Albertsons to Winn Dixie, carry a selection of fresh herbs, but because they're chains, they must follow a chain of command. The market manager frequently is powerless to buy from you even if you live next door and have the freshest herbs on earth—unless you can get

Smart Tip

Tip...

In addition to restaurant chefs, you can also target cooks at catering companies, upscale employee dining rooms, and swanky health centers.

▲

the home office to approve the deal. If you plan to sell to supermarkets, you'll need to add getting approval to your list of market research musts.

If you like the idea of old-fashioned market days in the town square or a monthly fair à la parsley, sage, rosemary, and thyme, get out your Renaissance garb and your market umbrella. Then rent a space at a local farmers' market or flea market and sell your freshly harvested herbs directly to consumers. Most towns run a farmers' market on a regular basis, from daily to once a week, while flea markets generally run two to four days a week.

These events are not only terrific sales venues but also a lot of fun. And while you're selling, you can initiate people into the joys of herbs—the more they know about your products, the more they're likely to buy.

Keeping It Contained

Another option is to sell your herbs in pots or other containers instead of selling them already cut. Customers range from small neighborhood nurseries to giant megalithic home improvement stores. You might sell a few of the better-known varieties of herbs like mint, basil, and dill, or you might fill out the store's shelves with a potpourri of more exotic types like comfrey and costmary. Superstore garden outlets can make good customers, but keep

Minding the Store

Herbal entrepreneurs often choose to open a retail shop, a wonderfully fragrant space bursting with herbs: fresh-picked, dried, and hung from the rafters, peering out of pots on the front steps, woven into wreaths, tacked onto recipe cards, infused into vinegars, and packaged into teas and potpourri. Most herb shops also sell other nature-themed products from other vendors, like books, candles, greeting cards, bath products, and clothing. You might locate your shop in a bustling downtown neighborhood or in a barn on your country farm.

Whichever way you go, keep in mind that a retail shop is a big responsibility that will keep you busy—and unless you hire help, tied to the store—during hours of operation and then some. And that's in addition to working your garden or farm.

But it can also be a lot of fun. You can supplement your income, as well as customers' interest, by hosting herb craft workshops (participants purchase supplies from you) and holiday open houses for events from Christmas to Midsummer's Eve.

in mind that, as with any other chain operation, you may have to woo the corporate office, as well as your local branch.

But don't stop with garden centers. Natural-food emporiums and health-food stores are good customers. And of course, farmers' markets and flea markets also provide terrific venues for selling container herbs.

You can sell your herbs in the quintessential plastic pots found at garden centers everywhere (and which are fantastically cheaper when purchased wholesale—see Chapter 8 for details) or in paper pots you make yourself out of recycled materials. Or get creative again and design your own fancy, functional, or just whimsical and fun containers from everything from old boots, teapots, and buckets to painted terra cotta urns. The right containers—even when made of recycled goods—can up the price of your herbs considerably.

You can also craft herb topiaries—elegant or fanciful creations made by training growing herbs up wire forms. Topiaries of all kinds are tremendously popular in the marketplace now, and herbal ones are even better.

Crafting Success

You can do so much more with herbs than simply selling fresh-cut sprigs and potted plants. If you're a creative type who loves working with styrofoam, raffia, ribbons, twine, and wire—and any other crafts materials—along with herbs and everlastings (dried flowers),

Tea Time

Atearoom or restaurant seems to be a natural extension of the herb farm. What better way, many growers decide, to show off their flavorful harvests than baked into a tantalizing assortment of dishes? The tearoom can share space with your shop—provided you get approval from your local health inspector.

And it can add a tidy amount to your income. Besides feeding customers a dainty selection of tea cakes and sandwiches, you can expand to holiday or more frequent luncheons or dinners of heartier herbal fare from stews and salmon to roast beast. You might also host herbal cooking classes and herb lectures followed by herb feasts, all of which will have diners clamoring to buy your herbs for their own kitchens.

Like the retail shop, however, the tea room or restaurant can be extremely time-consuming and an expensive start-up. Consider it carefully before you leap in.

Bright Idea

Landscape architects and contractors can be a terrific market for one of the newest trends in landscaping—using hardy herbs like rosemary and oregano in place of boring, less aromatic and more maintenance-heavy old standbys.

then you'll be in your element. You can make herb wreaths, centerpieces, swags, dream pillows, potpourri, stationery, candles, corsages, boutonnieres, and bridal bouquets, as well as any other herb craft you can dream up.

You'll have a wide choice of sales outlets as well. You can sell direct to consumers at flea markets and arts and crafts festivals or sell the Mary Kay or Tupperware way at home parties. Sell by mail using catalogs and/or a Web site. Sell from your own shop, either on your farm or at a retail location in town. Or go wholesale by selling to retailers from home décor shops to gift boutiques and consignment crafts shops.

The Herbal Apothecary

Creating with herbs doesn't have to be limited to fashioning wreaths and other home décor items. There's also an abundant and thriving market for herbal bath and beauty products of every description. You can craft your own line of soaps, shampoos, bath oils, bubbles, salts, lotions, creams, scrubs, splashes, and fragrances. Add in-room spritzers to cleanse and scent the air, linen sprays (aromatherapy for your bed sheets and pillowcases), and even ironing mists for infusing fresh laundry with herbal scents while you press.

You can also design your own line of green, or environmentally safe and sound, housecleaning products, from glass and mirror sprays to gentle but effective kitchen and bath cleansers and furniture polishes. These home-care items are as yet far less popular than bath and beauty lines, but turn the pages of any home-oriented magazine and you'll notice a steady tide of articles on the dangers of chemicals in store-bought cleaning products and the delights of making your own healthy ones.

If you're a culinary artist, more at home with a spatula and a wooden spoon than a hot glue gun and glitter, you might turn your herbal creativity to goodies from the kitchen. You can bottle oils and vinegars made with fresh herbs. Package your own secret blends of dried herbs to be used as the bases for chip dips, soups, salad dressings, cookies, and desserts. Or develop your own line of herbal teas, designed not only for taste but also to aid in sweet dreams, caffeine-free good mornings, stress relief, or clear thinking and more.

Sell your line of herbal apothecaries or culinary creations the same way you'd sell other herb crafts—at fairs and festivals, through home shows, by mail, wholesale, or retail at your own outlet or on the Internet.

Bright Idea

Target party, bridal, and event planners, as well as florists as markets for fresh-cut and potted herbs—what better way to say the special things like love and remembrance than through the language and beauty of herbs?

A Nice Niche

As you target your market, start thinking market niche. This is your special corner of the market, the area of expertise and interest that makes your herbal business stand out from the crowd and the competition.

Your niche might be one of the following:

Bright Idea

Don't forget Fido and Boots! Pets can benefit from herbal baths, conditioners, and flea deterrents along with perennially popular catnip toys. Since animals react differently to some herbs than people do, so check with a veterinarian to make sure your potential products are pet-safe.

- *Herbal products for kids.* Craft bubbling baths, shampoos, dream pillows, and more for the set that really knows how to make bathtime fun. Keep in mind that little humans can be more sensitive to herbs and oils than adults—check with a pediatrician when formulating your products.

- *Fairy garden herbs.* Fairies, elves, and other magical garden sprites are very popular these days. Create herbal apothecaries and crafts (even fairy abodes!) with a flower fairy theme.

- *Herbal therapy for the office.* Give the workplace—and all those corporate 9-to-5ers in it—an herbal lift with apothecaries, crafts, and container plants designed to transform Dilbert-type cubicles into havens of delight.

- *Rare or exotic herbs.* If there are lots of growers in your area raising mint and basil, you might plant yourself as the farmer who sells, say, bergamot, lady's bedstraw, comfrey, vervain, and germander.

- *Year-round herb supplier.* If most of the herb suppliers in your region sell only during the growing season, you might invest in a greenhouse and develop a reputation as the grower with fresh herbs even in the heart of winter.

- *Landscape herb supplier.* You may decide to specialize in companion plants, those that gardeners buy not only for their scent, texture, and good looks, but because they act as natural pest controls in the garden.

- *Healing herb supplier.* You may choose to specialize in herbs from the ancient physick garden, as well as plants with newly rediscovered health benefits.

- *Fresh and organic.* No matter what other niche you develop, you'll want to use the fact that your herbs are fresh from the garden and organically grown as your calling card—it's your best feature and finest selling point.

Smart Tip

Tip...

If you plan to market your own line of herbal culinary delights, talk with the people at the National Association for the Specialty Food Trade. You'll find contact information in the appendix at the back of this book.

Bright Idea

Fragrance gardens, butterfly gardens, and hummingbird gardens are very popular. Why not specialize in herbs for these special gardens? You can not only sell the botanicals, but also help customers design their yards.

What to Grow?

For further insight into how to choose herbs for your garden, take some tips from the experts. The herbal entrepreneurs we interviewed for this book base their garden plans on their particular niches, growing the botanicals that suit their customers' needs.

"We're always on the lookout for new varieties of herbs," says Michele, the herb farmer in Soddy Daisy, Tennessee. "I'm propagating the new lavender mint for spring and will be carrying several varieties of sage. We grow all our herbs from cuttings and seed. I have several varieties of scented geraniums, rosemary, thyme, lemon grass, mints, chives, anise, hyssop, lavender, artemisia (silver king), lemon balm, and basil. We provide the commonly grown herbs for someone just getting started and hopefully provide something a little different for the herb gardener looking for something new."

Cindy has her own garden plan for her Texas herb farm. "I grow a variety of the common culinary herbs such as mint, rosemary, oregano, thyme, sage, basil, and marjoram," she explains. "I try to stock many of the different cultivars of these herbs, such as ginger mint, orange mint, lemon thyme, silver thyme, purple sage, Thai basil, cinnamon basil, and purple ruffled basil.

"My specialty really is to carry lots of the uncommon herbs that may not be as familiar to many people for cooking but are useful in other ways such as for tea, craft work, landscaping, or even medicinally. Some of these include horehound, chamomile, a

The Last Resort

Some herb farms develop—either by design or popular demand—as tourist destinations, country resorts where visitors can stroll through gardens, visit gift shops and tearooms, listen to lectures, attend workshops, or even spend a night in an herbal bed and breakfast. This, of course, is the herb farm on a grand scale, with far more than herb raising to keep the owner and a dozen or more employees busy day and night. If this is your plan, go for it—but be sure you've thoroughly investigated every avenue.

If you're a major people person, you may find a steady stream of visitors an exhilarating prospect. But if you're not, the idea of a constant weekend house party can be daunting if not downright draining.

Brazilian plant simply called cinnamon bush (great for tea), soapwort (or Bouncing Bet), Gotu Kola, prunella (or Self-Heal), and comfrey, just to name a few."

But Cindy doesn't stop there—her herbal acre produces lots more. "As with many businesses, it's important to diversify," she advises. "So in addition to herbs, I also raise and sell—both wholesale and retail—a selection of heirloom and open-pollinated vegetable seedlings in season. In the spring, tomatoes, peppers, eggplant, and some squash and cucumbers are available. In late summer, I have tomatoes and eggplant again, as well as peppers. Then in fall, I have a great selection of lettuces, various broccoli, Asian greens, kale, and other varieties of greens that overwinter here in our Texas climate. A selection of vines, perennials, and Texas natives is also available."

Do Your Homework

Once you've decided on what sort of herbs you want to grow, what—if any—herbal products you'll create, and who you'll sell them to, you can plan a strategy for researching your market to make sure it's large enough to support your efforts. There are all sorts of ways to go about this, from gathering statistics to taking surveys.

One popular way to research your market is by going direct to the source and querying potential customers with a focus group. Here you invite anywhere from five to 12 people to participate and then bombard them with questions. Of course, you don't just yank people in off the street—you choose carefully. If you plan to sell dried herbs and everlastings to crafters, for instance, you'd invite members of local crafts clubs. If you'll specialize in herbs for pets and their people, you'll invite members of local kennel associations or dog obedience classes.

Once you've assembled your group—or groups, if you plan to hold more than one focus session—you can offer them some sort of refreshment (herbal, of course!) and hand out your questionnaires along with pencils for filling them in. Take a look at the "Sample Focus Group Questionnaire" on page 57, then formulate your own based on your products and your target market. Ask as many questions as you feel your group can handle and encourage discussion. You'll learn lots!

Survey Says

Another surefire way to ascertain the size and interest level of your target market is via direct-mail surveys. Here, you send questionnaires to the people you believe will make up your ideal audience and forthrightly ask them their buying preferences and habits.

If you belong to an association, organization, or listserv, and it just happens to be affiliated

Bright Idea

Don't leave out Italian eateries and pizza parlors in your quest for restaurants to do business with. Garlic, basil, and oregano are the hallmarks of Italian cuisine.

Bright Idea

Target holistic health practitioners or medicinal herb wholesalers as customers for your fresh or dried herbs. Keep in mind that they may want to view your farm and have proof of organic certification before taking you on as a supplier.

with your target market (like crafters for those dried herbs or a culinary society for the fresh-picked stuff), you've got it made. You may already have a directory packed with names and phone numbers at hand. If not, you may be able to beg, borrow, or buy a directory from the organization's main office. You can also buy batches of names from list brokers who specialize in supplying lists for just about every interest group in existence. Prices run about $50 per 1,000 names. (For more on list brokers, see Chapter 12.)

What should you ask? Check out the "Sample Direct-Mail Market Research Survey," which consists of a cover letter and a one-page survey, on pages 55 and 56. Your queries will relate to your own target market and products, but you can use this as a starting point for what and how to ask.

Another way to query those potential customers is through telephone surveys, which are basically the same as direct-mail or listserv surveys. The advantage to the telephone survey over direct mail is that you don't have to worry that your mailing will end up in the wastebasket. Once you've got your potential customer on the phone, you can ask away and jot down those answers.

The big disadvantage, of course, is that in an era when telemarketers seem to be driving everybody crazy with unsolicited calls, you may be perceived in the same fashion. But

Trend Tracking

Are there any trendy "new" herbs you should consider for your new venture? "I'd look into growing Chinese and ayurvedic [an ancient Hindu medical practice and philosophy] herbs because that market is just opening," advises Maureen Rogers president of the Herb Growing and Marketing Network. "If it's pushed in the media, it's already too late."

"It really depends on the focus of your business," says Cindy M., vice president of the Texas Herb Growers and Marketers Association. "Since I sell plants, I try to sell the common and the unusual. I like to grow the medicinal herbs as 'oddities' so people can see and grow the products they might be taking in capsule or pill form. I keep track of the popular scents and culinary trends, too. For instance, lavender has made a tremendous jump in the culinary market, while rosemary, oregano, and some of the other hardy herbs have come into their own as landscape plants."

Tip...

Smart Tip

People are unlikely to return a mail survey unless you offer them an incentive. So get creative! Give them a coupon for 10 percent off their first order. This gives you a head start on advanced sales and also helps spread the word about your products—and word-of-mouth sells.

if you can use the mailing lists we explored in the direct-mail section above, you have a foot in the door. Your call won't seem unsolicited if you can say that you belong to the Maricopa Chapter of the Crafters League or the Eastern Shore Culinary Society or whatever—or that your brother, sister, spouse, or child does. For ideas on what to ask, see the "Sample Telephone Market Research Survey" on page 54.

Just the Stats

Besides going directly to your potential customers for your market research, you'll also want cool, calculated statistics—facts like the number of arthritis sufferers there are in the United States for those mail order

Growing Strong

Get to the root of the herb business by joining trade organizations. The International Herb Association, the American Botanical Council, and the Herb Growing and Marketing Network all exist for the sole purpose of helping herb farmers and marketers grow strong. When you become a member, you get advice from experts in the industry on starting your business, as well as growing it once you're up and running. Make contacting trade organizations a priority on your list of market research must-dos.

"At first I just jumped right in," Texas Herb Growers and Marketers Association vice president Cindy M. says of her market research efforts. "Then, over the first winter, I did some research to find more outlets such as farmers' markets, sponsored herb shows, and a few retail customers. I joined a national herb organization and a statewide organization as well. There I met and could talk to others in the business, go to conferences and learn from 'the professionals.' I read everything I could about herbs, herb growing, and the herb business."

Michele B. in Soddy Daisy, Tennessee, agrees. "We're members of the Herb Growing and Marketing Network," she says, "which is very helpful to herb businesses, providing many services from free advertising to discussion boards and Web hosting."

You'll find contact information on the herb organizations listed above—plus more—in the appendix at the back of this book.

healing herbs, or how many upscale restaurants there are in your city for your fresh-cut herb deliveries.

The answers to questions like these will help you determine just how many prospective customers you can expect and whether that number is large enough to be lucrative. Where do you get all this statistical stuff? Try these terrific sources:

- *Hit the books.* Pay your local reference librarian a visit and explain what you need to know—and why. Tell her that you need to know how many craft shops there are in the Midwest, how many herb wholesalers are in the greater Seattle area, or how many adults with arthritis there are in the United States. She'll provide you with stacks of demographic statistics with more facts and figures than you thought could possibly exist.

- *Get on the Net.* You'll find all sorts of answers on the Internet. For starters, go to your local city or chamber of commerce Web site, which may supply you with information on restaurants and markets. For less regional material, like where to find crafters around the country, click on any number of general and specialized search engines, from Yahoo! and Google to InfoJump.

- *Check out the organization.* Sometimes the best place to go for information on a target market is the group's organization. If your market is crafters, for instance, you'd contact the National Craft Association and the Association of Crafts and Creative Industries for counts of their members.

Beware!
Never, ever try to pin down a chef with market research or any other kinds of questions during peak meal times. All you'll get is a cranky, overstressed person—and no answers to your questions. Inquire instead during slower hours when she'll have time to devote to you rather than that five-star entrée on the back burner.

Herbal Rivalry

While you're doing your market research, don't forget to check out what sort of competition your business will face. Depending on which niche you choose, your rivals may take the form of other herb farms, herbal health and beauty product purveyors, herbal crafts suppliers, home décor stores, or herb wholesalers.

Not to panic here—a little competition is healthy. If you do your homework properly and structure your niche wisely, your company will shine despite your rivals' qualities.

"In this business, it's possible to have two herb growers in the same community," says Michele, whose farm is about 20 miles north of Chattanooga, Tennessee. "Each business usually does something just a little different and always helps the other by giving out their names, Web sites, etc. I researched this area before we moved and found that there wasn't any type of herb farm 50 miles in either direction. There are some garden centers, but they only sell a few herbs and nothing fancy."

Your own market research phase is the time to scrutinize any rivals. Ask the following questions:

- What are they doing that works?
- What can I successfully copy?
- What are they doing that I can do better?
- What can I offer that will draw customers away from them and to me?

You can answer these questions by performing the following research tasks:

- *Go ahead, shop the competition!* Go into groceries, markets, or crafts stores and look at the herbal products offered. Study the quality of the herbs and the way they're displayed. Talk to employees and find out how often new products are brought in.

- *If you plan to go mail order, send for every mail order catalog you can find featuring herbal products similar to the ones you plan to offer.* Study them to determine what specific products they offer, in what quantities and at what prices.

- *Surf those Internet sites of herbal business similar to yours.* Again, study what your rivals are doing, and explore what works and what doesn't.

Smart Tip

Tip...

As an herbal entrepreneur, you're also an herbal ambassador. Part of your job is to educate your customers about the benefits and uses of botanicals. They'll enjoy learning—and they'll buy more products.

Sample Telephone Market Research Survey

Questionnaire for Busy Chefs

1. How many times a week do you order fresh-picked herbs? _____

2. How many times a week would you like to be able to order fresh herbs? _____

3. Which of the following herbs do you use on a weekly or more frequent basis?
   ❑ Basil ❑ Mint ❑ Thyme ❑ Cilantro ❑ Rosemary ❑ Parsley

4. Which of the following herbs would you like to be able to use on a regular basis?
   ❑ Sage ❑ French Tarragon ❑ Chervil ❑ Lavender ❑ Lemon Balm

5. Please list any other fresh herbs you'd like to cook with but don't currently have access to: _____

   _____

6. Which of the following edible flowers would you like to be able to use on a regular basis?
   ❑ Rose Petals ❑ Pansies ❑ Nasturtiums ❑ Violets ❑ Chamomile

7. Do you currently order from a local herb grower or from a wholesaler or distributor? _____

8. What do you like best about your current fresh-herb purveyor (i.e., quantity, freshness, appearance, variety, price, customer service)?

   _____

   _____

9. What do you like least about your current fresh-herb purveyor (i.e., quantity, freshness, appearance, variety, price, customer service)?

   _____

   _____

Sample Direct-Mail Market Research Survey

Thyme Out Herb Farm
Give Yourself the Gift of Time

How would you like to be able to take time out from today's hectic world whenever you like? Take time to enjoy the simple things in life, to relax and live with the rhythm of the seasons, to pamper yourself and those around you with soothing scents and sensibilities?

Sound too wonderful to be true? Not so! Let Thyme Out Herb Farm's herbal pot-pourri, dream pillows, room misters, lotions, and soaps transport you to a quiet, relaxing and rejuvenating world where there's always plenty of time. I'd like to offer you a special gift just for trying our handcrafted herbal treasures.

But first, I need your help. To tailor our products to your needs and desires, I'm asking you to fill out the enclosed questionnaire and send it back. It's a self-mailer, so it's easy! To show my appreciation, once I've received your answers, I'll send you a coupon for 10 percent off any Thyme Out products purchased on our Web site or at the farm.

Sound exciting? It is! When you visit us on the Internet or here at the farm, you'll be thrilled with the quality of our products. Not only are they as wonderfully scented, refreshing, and relaxing as you'd expect, but they also come in very Victorian and whimsical packages that make them a delight to give as gifts— or to keep all for yourself... if you can! Your friends will clamor to know where you got them!

- So fill out the questionnaire.
- Send it back.
- And get ready to take a Thyme Out.

Yours in Thyme,

Sorrel Seabrook

168 Thyme Creek Road, Cottage Garden, GA 40500
(440) 555-0000, www.thymeoutherbs.com

▲

Thyme Out Herb Farm

Help Us Design the Herbal Products You Desire

What is your favorite time of day to unwind and relax?
❏ Morning ❏ Midafternoon ❏ Early evening ❏ Late at night

What is your most hectic period of the day?
❏ Morning ❏ Midafternoon ❏ Early evening ❏ Late at night

Tell us what type of work you do: _____

How many people are in your household? _____

What are their ages? _____

What is your age range? ❏ 18–25 ❏ 26–35 ❏ 36–45 ❏ 46–65 ❏ 66 and over

Which of these areas do you find yourself coping with the most
during a typical day?
❏ Stress ❏ Anxiety ❏ Tiredness ❏ Boredom

What is your favorite way to unwind and relax?
❏ Warm bath ❏ Soft music ❏ Gardening ❏ Long walk
❏ Good book ❏ Cooking ❏ Crafting ❏ Other: _____

Would you be interested in purchasing and growing your own
container herbs? _____

What is your annual household income? _____

About how much do you spend each month on personal-care products
(bath and body oils and lotions, shampoos, fragrances, etc.)?
❏ under $25 ❏ $26 to $50 ❏ $50 and up

Sample Focus Group Questionnaire

1. How many times a year do you purchase bath and body products like lotions, fragrances, and bath oils for yourself? _____

2. How many times a year do you purchase bath and body products like lotions, fragrances, and bath oils as gifts? _____

3. How much do you usually spend on these items for yourself? _____

4. How much do you usually spend when purchasing these items as gifts? _____

5. How many times a year do you purchase gift baskets to give as gifts? _____

6. How much do you usually spend per gift basket? _____

7. For which special occasions do you purchase bath and body products as gifts? _____

8. For which special occasions do you purchase gift baskets? _____

9. Would you buy a 4-ounce jar of Lavender & Lemon Stress Relief Bath Salts? *(Here you show the product to your group.)* _____

10. How much would you expect to pay for this product? _____

11. Would you purchase a 6-ounce bottle of Lavender & Lemon Stress Relief Room Spritzer? *(Here you show the product to your group.)* _____

12. How much would you expect to pay for this product? _____

13. How many times in the past year have you purchased a product by mail order or via the Internet? _____

14. Were you pleased with your purchase? _____

15. If so, why? _____

16. If not, why not? _____

17. How many times in the past year have you purchased a product at a specialty shop or boutique that was not in the mall? (This means a small independently owned shop; Wal-Mart, supermarkets, and other chain retailers don't count.) _____

18. Please comment on the name Thyme Out Herb Farm (love, like, dislike, or hate and why). _____

19. Please comment on the name Chamomile Creek Herb Farm (love, like, dislike, or hate and why) _____

The North 40

Your Farm Location

It seems fairly obvious: If you're going to operate an herb farm, you need a *farm*, a country spread miles from civilization with only cows, horses, and the occasional pig for neighbors. Right? Not necessarily.

You can successfully grow commercial herbs just about anywhere these days—on a city lot, in a suburban backyard, or on that traditional country acreage. And it works in just about any location in the nation. Herb farmers report tremendous success in climes as different as Arizona and Minnesota.

In this chapter, we'll explore how to decide whether your present location will work as an herb business, how to scout out the perfect new location, and how to deal with governmental issues like zoning and building permits.

Photo© PhotoDisc Inc.

Herbs in the 'Burbs

If you live in the city or the suburbs, you may already have the ideal site for the start-up herb farm. You won't need a lot of growing room at first, so a backyard or a rooftop garden can fill in just fine for that rural acreage.

In fact, you've got one big advantage over the country herb farm: close proximity to prospective customers. You won't have to go far afield to find—and serve—a bevy of restaurant, market, and retail buyers for your herbal products. In contrast, the rural farmer has to think long and hard about where she'll find her customer base and how she'll supply it.

Of course, not all urban and suburban locations are alike, so you'll still have to do that market research to determine if your location is right for the herb farm you plan. If you live in a depressed area where upscale eateries are few and far between and folks are struggling to put bread on the table, you won't find much of a market for seeming frivolities like French tarragon and pineapple sage. But if your town is bursting with trendy restaurants and prosperous garden centers, you should get off to a great start.

So just what is the perfect urban or suburban herb farm? The number of plants you choose to start with and the design you prefer is basically up to you, but you'll want to take the following into consideration:

- *Size matters—sort of.* Your 'burb herb farm doesn't have to encompass 40 acres, but you will need enough land

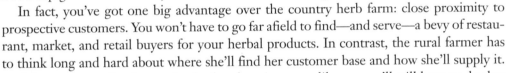

Smart Tip

Tip...

Raised beds made of block or timbers filled in with good growing soil can make excellent urban "farmland." The height of the beds—2 to 3 feet off the ground—saves wear and tear on your back and knees. And the fact that you mix your own soil instead of working with what's underfoot means you start with the best base for your plants.

to grow a profitable number of plants. You can add to your square footage by terracing a slope, tucking herbs in among other plantings, and taking advantage of nontraditional crop areas like your front yard or a side yard tucked between your house and a neighbor's.

- *Shady characters.* Most herbs are sun lovers, but some, like bee balm, chamomile, and thyme, are just as happy in the shade. Take into account any neighboring homes or offices that block the sun for most of the day; then plan for your garden's sunny or shady characteristics and choose herbs that match.

- *The root zone.* Some suburban settings boast mature trees, which make beautiful landscape features but not good neighbors for herbs. Make sure your garden doesn't come too close to trees' root zones—digging around roots can injure the trees, and those same roots can leach nutrients and water away from the herbs.

Location Scout

If you live in a city apartment with not even a fire escape on which to grow plants or your suburban backyard is just too small, you've still got alternatives that don't include moving to the country.

For starters, scout out vacant lots, whether tucked between office buildings or languishing on a corner overrun with weeds. You'll often find properties no one else wants because their neighbors are less-than-desirable businesses like auto salvage yards or fish

Permit Me

If you'll be building a greenhouse, tool shed, barn, or other structure, you'll need to get another piece of paper from the G-men in your city or county: a building permit. Don't ignore this with the idea that if you don't ask, you won't get told on. Sooner or later, somebody in authority will find your pretty new greenhouse or barn and come asking questions. If you don't have a permit, you'll either have to apply for one after the fact and pay sometimes stiff penalties, or be forced to tear it down. So be smart and get permission before you build.

processing plants. You can also look for the odd residential lot that never got built on—the forlorn one sprouting dandelions and nettles between homes and lawns.

When you find one with potential, locate the owner by checking with the city or county property tax office. Contact him and negotiate a low rent. Point out that under your stewardship, his empty land will not only bring in rent but will be nurtured and beautified. Instead of an urban beacon to trash dumpers and other vandals and a possible target for city code enforcement officials, it will enhance the neighborhood.

You can also consider leasing land that lays fallow beneath a grid of power lines from your local power company. Prolonged exposure to EMF (or electromagnetic field) waves aren't recommended for people, but plants seem to love them. You can often lease this land inexpensively—the rent you pay is gravy for the power company, which is already using the land to its own capacity. It helps beautify the area, a PR point for the power people. And again, no one else is likely to want it; with those electrical towers in the way, you couldn't build on it. So go negotiate!

Out in the Sticks

If you choose to locate your herb business in a rural setting, you're looking at a whole different set of parameters. You'll be living the dream of countless thousands of unhappy

On Display

If you have the space—and the disposition for visitors—a display garden is an excellent way to promote your products. "My display gardens are very important to me," says Cindy M. in Hallettsville, Texas, "because they show the customer how mature herbs and other plants look in the landscape, which plants look good together, and how plants look at different times of the year." Along with her display gardens, Cindy stocks an array of retail products to help customers nurture their own herbs, such as potting soil, pots, and organic fertilizers. "I also have a small selection of books on herbs, herb gardening, and cooking to help people get started with the herbs they purchase," she explains.

Michele B.'s display gardens in Soddy Daisy, Tennessee, serve a similar purpose. "We have display gardens that come into their own during early summer and again in the fall," she says. She and husband Scott also have plans for a shop. "Right now we're selling and growing from our greenhouse, which works well with customers," she says. "This summer I plan to put tables under that big live oak and offer a shady spot for customers to browse."

slaves of the rat race—to toss in the towel on the 9-to-5 world and move to the country, where the pace is slower, the air is cleaner, and life is sweeter.

But before you sell the house and pack the car, carefully consider that rural paradise. Will your farm have a large enough customer base to support it (and you)? How far will you have to drive to make deliveries to restaurants or other customers?

One way to have your herbal cake and eat it too is to relocate to a semirural location, say an hour or less from a major metropolitan area. Look for subdivisions laid out with equestrian activities or minifarms in mind. These typically consist of half-acre to two-acre home sites where you can have a stable, corral, chicken coop or even a barn out behind your home. There's plenty of land to start a good-sized herb farm and still be city-close. If your spouse or significant other wants to work in town while you run the farm, he or she can commute in.

Smart Tip

Tip...

If you're out in the country, it's important to include a map in all brochures and other sales materials, even on your Web site. "We recommend that visitors driving out to us call for directions—we haven't lost anyone yet!" says herbal entrepreneur Michele B. in Soddy Daisy, Tennessee.

Some of these tracts—designed for the upscale horse set—can carry upscale price tags. Others, designed for folks more interested in the full farm experience complete with homegrown pumpkins and pigs than membership in the equestrian club, are more reasonably priced. Check out the areas near you for one that might suit your priorities and your budget.

Tourist Traps

If your rural area is on the tourist trail, peppered here and there with charming villages, scenic wonders, or historic sites, then you've got a potentially terrific locale for a destination herb farm. You can tempt customers off the beaten path and down your driveway to ooh, ahh, browse, and ultimately buy.

"We're on National Park Loop 101," says Mike R., the lavender grower in Sequim, Washington. "We applied for freeway directional signs, and we get 500 to 1,000 people per day on the farm."

"We're in a very rural area," says herb grower Cindy M. in Hallettsville, Texas, "about eight miles from two towns of about 2,700 people each. Houston and San Antonio are each about 100 miles away, and Austin is about 80 miles. We're not an area that really attracts tourists, but we do get lots of people traveling through to the Gulf Coast in the fall and back up north again in the spring. These people sometimes stay at local RV parks and can be looking for something to do during a break from their travels. Many come shop and take herbs home with them."

Now, if you have your heart set on living way out in the real country (or you really live there), far from a metropolitan center and miles from anything tourists might be remotely

Tip...

Smart Tip

Shops and restaurants located in summertime tourist areas often close in the off-season. This can coincide nicely with the end of your growing season, relieving you of worries about not being able to supply customers in the winter.

interested in, you can still run a successful operation. But you'll probably have to go either wholesale and ship your products long distances or go the mail-order version of retail.

The big advantage you'll have over your more customer-based competition is that you'll have land—lots of land—to grow as much as you like. And of course, the further out you go, generally the less expensive that land is to purchase. So do your homework and your market research before you start site shopping.

The Ideal Site

If you plan to start your herb farm on land you already own, be it your suburban backyard or a country spread, you'll work with what you've got; poor soil can be amended and lack of water can be mitigated with irrigation. But if you're moving to new digs to start your farm, you'll want to consider the following elements:

- *Super soil.* Good soil makes good plants. The better the soil on your farm, the less time, effort and money you'll have to spend amending it. Look for good loam with natural drainage—herbs don't like hanging around with wet roots in soggy dirt. Sandy soil is not a plus because it will require more water and more nutrients. And while some herbs like a bit of clay, all-clay soil is not a plus either—it's sticky, unyielding, and will require lots of amendments.

- *Clear water.* Is the water source clear and clean or will you face problems from upstream or groundwater toxins? Remember that your main claim to fame is organic, pesticide-free products, which you can't get if your water doesn't have the same clean qualities. You'll also want to ask about drought conditions—if there's no water to be had from Mother Nature and the local government has banned watering, you'll be hoeing several tough rows.

- *Weather or not to plant.* There are successful herb growers in hot and humid Louisiana, ice-bound Minnesota and arid Arizona, but climate still plays a big part in growing activities. Will your farm have an adequate growing season or will you need to install a greenhouse to stretch out your spring and fall?

- *The right site.* Look for a site that's flat, well-drained, yet high and dry. A farm that's located in a flood plain, high on a windy hill, or in a microclimate that gets either too much or not enough rain will have a hard time nurturing healthy plants.

- *Growing room.* If you're taking the major breathtaking step of buying land, you'll want to stay put where you're planted. Make sure you've got room to expand your operations as your business grows so you don't have to uproot and move after a few years.

- *Storability.* You'll want space to stash your equipment and supplies, from transplant pots to rototillers. And if you make herbal products, you'll have workbenches and other equipment and supplies to store.

- *Previous incarnation.* Ask what the land you're exploring has previously been used for. If it's been heavily dosed with pesticides or other toxins, you may want to look elsewhere.

- *Barn none.* If you plan a retail operation like a shop or tea room or a manufacturing concern for herbal products, is there an existing barn or other building that can be converted, or will you have to build from scratch? What will renovations or a new structure cost?

- *Ins and outs.* Will customers be able to get in and out of your farm easily? Check to see that the drive doesn't exit onto a major thoroughfare with speeding traffic that will have people risking their lives as they come and go. Or—perhaps as dangerous—is it filled with hairpin turns that will have customers spinning off mountainsides?

Use our handy "Location, Location Checklist" on page 67 when you're scouting out your ideal farm.

<table>
<tr><td>

Tip...

Smart Tip

Get expert assistance in determining soil type and pH from the local county extension service or from independent soil consultants. You'll find the latter in the local Yellow Pages, on the Internet or in ads in herb trade and gardening publications.

</td></tr>
</table>

Talking Shop

If you're considering a retail shop, you're probably planning to include it as part of your herb farm or gardens, which means that unlike most other retail operators, you don't need to spend time scouting out sites at the neighborhood mall or strip shopping center. But depending on your location, zoning regulations, or other special situations, you may opt to go with an off-farm shop. This will tend to add a lot of complications to your operation. You'll have travel time from farm to store and back to factor in. And of course, you'll have double the bills, including rent, utilities, and phone.

If you decide to go for an off-site shop, you'll want to choose your location as carefully as you do your farm. Take these tips in hand while you scout:

- *Shopping mall.* You should probably skip these, as rents are astronomical and typically require that you pay a percentage of your profits to the lessor. Leases may stipulate that you spring for a major remodel of your shop every few years.

- *Historic storefront.* Consider a storefront in an historic district or quaint and quirky downtown. Large cities and small towns alike often have recently ratty neighborhoods that are being revitalized to become a shopper's haven.

- *All-in-one.* Aim for a retail location that includes some land that will allow you to have your farm and shop together in town. Look for sites like small suburban garden centers, which

> **Smart Tip**
>
> Read up on all the answers on retail operations in Entrepreneur's business start-up *Start Your Own Retail Store.*

already have land for growing; day-care centers, which usually include an outdoor play area; or a shop with temporary buildings like sheds that can be torn down.

Zoning Out

No matter where you locate your farm, you'll need to check the local zoning regulations to find out if you can legally run your commercial garden in your chosen spot. If you plan a backyard herb farm, for instance, you may discover that your town prohibits operating a business in a residential area. Or you may learn that you can't operate an agricultural concern on a city lot.

If this turns out to be true, don't panic. You can often get a variance—a special permit just for you—simply by applying for it. You may have to appear at a civic planning meeting to explain your farm and its low impact on the neighborhood, but that's OK—it's a terrific opportunity to talk about the beauty of herbs and their positive value in your locale.

City and county zoning-code people are also concerned about parking issues—and so are the neighbors. No one wants to have their street clogged with cars double-parked on the grass or edging into neighboring driveways. If this will be a problem at your farm, think of how you'll get around it before you confront the planning committee. Can you pave part of your front yard for extra parking? Add extra parking spaces on the verge of your city lot? Or get a signed petition from your neighbors showing that they're not opposed to a few extra cars on the street?

> **Smart Tip**
>
> A retail herb business generally needs less land than does a wholesale one. Why? Wholesale herbs are sold for half the price of retail and in large quantities, while retail sales consist of a few plants or fresh-cut herbs per customer.

Yet another issue you'll want to check out with the zoning code enforcement people is signage. If you'll run a strictly wholesale or mail order operation with no walk-in customers, you won't need to worry about signs. But if you plan any sort of retail trade, you'll want a sign to advertise your presence and perhaps another to show people where to park. Most cities and counties have ordinances

Location, Location Checklist

Use this worksheet as you shop for the best location for your herb farm. Even if you plan to stick to home base instead of buying acreage, use this sheet to decide if weather, site, and local ordinances will make your farm feasible. Make copies and use one sheet for each possible location.

1. What are the soil conditions? _____

2. Is the water toxin-free? _____

3. Is drought an issue? _____

4. When does natural growing start and end? _____

5. What is the climate? _____

6. What is the microclimate, if any? _____

7. Is there room to grow? _____

8. Is there adequate storage and work space? _____

9. What was the land previously used for? _____

10. Are there existing structures that can be used? _____

11. What will be the cost of renovations or new structures? _____

12. Will customers be able to get in and out of the farm easily? _____

13. Is the site zoned for farming? _____

14. If not, can you get a variance? _____

15. Will parking be an issue? _____

16. Will signage be an issue? _____

17. Will you need a building permit? _____

regulating the areas in which signs are allowed, the manner in which they can be displayed (freestanding, on buildings or on banners), and even what size, materials and colors they can be. Be sure to check before you have signs made.

The Preowned Farm

An alternative to starting your herb farm from scratch is to buy an existing operation, complete with equipment, inventory, and supplies. This can be either a splendid investment or a disaster in the making. If the current owner is selling a prosperous business because of poor health, a family crisis, or because he's won $10 million and is moving to the south of France, you've got a good chance at continuing his success. But if he's selling because he just couldn't make a go of it, beware. He may have tried to buck an unfavorable location or hefty local competition—and you'll be stuck with the same obstacles.

How do you find out what you're getting into? Ask lots of questions, like these:

- What are the soil, water, and weather conditions?
- What's the competition like?
- What are the farm's financial records? Ask to see statements for the current and last three years, as well as his actual sales tax records.
- What's the customer volume like? Hang out on the farm for a few days and monitor daily customers and sales.
- Is the equipment in good condition or simply a liability to be hauled to the landfill?
- Will you need to add so many new crops and irrigation systems that you'd do just as well or better to start out on your own?
- What about inventory? Is it stuff you can actually use or sell or more candidates for the landfill?
- Can he show permits for any greenhouses, barns, or other outbuildings?

Preparing the Soil
Legal Structure and Physical Layout

Just as you have to root a seed or cutting before you get a strong, healthy herb plant, you also have to root your business before you'll have a strong, healthy, and successful herb enterprise. This means expending the time and effort (and yes, funds) to develop a sound business structure—both physically and legally. In this chapter, we'll explore what it takes

▲

to lay a solid foundation, from office location and company image to dealing with Uncle Sam and choosing a legal structure.

Image Makers

Image is important—and it's not just an issue for actors, rock stars, and politicians. Part of having a successful herb business is developing an image, whether it's as a down-home supplier of herbal remedies, an upscale supplier of trendy edibles, or anything in between. A large part of your image is the colors, graphics, typefaces, and paper stocks you choose for everything from stationery and mailing labels to hang tags for your products.

If you'll sell culinary herbs, for instance, you might design a logo that features basils and oreganos dancing alongside a chef's salad tongs to embellish your company name. If you'll specialize in dried herbs for crafters, you might go with a country crafts theme of folk-art angels bearing armfuls of Sweet Annie.

Name that Herb Business

Naming your herb business is one of the most fun—and most important—aspects of establishing your company image. It's an element that will immediately identify you and your herbs, whether you sell at a farmers' market, on the Internet, to retail customers, or strictly to the wholesale trade.

You can choose any name you like that doesn't already belong to somebody else. It's a good idea, however, not to get too specific. If you call your farm The Mint Patch because you only grow mint and then decide later to branch out to other herbs as well, you may find you've painted yourself into an herbal corner. The same may occur if you call your culinary herb gardens something like Chefs' Best Herbs and decide to branch out later to medicinal or crafts plants. Remember, one of the keys to staying successful in the herb business is to be able to go with the flow of popular crops.

You might want to add the words "Herb Farm" to your company name, you may choose to go with "Herb Gardens," or you may decide on something entirely different, like North Woods Herb Cabin or Anna's Herb Adobe.

If you're at a loss for potential names, try these brainstorming ideas:

- You could name your company after a noteworthy scenic or meteorologic feature of your area, like Seaside Cliffs Herb Gardens or Fog City Herb Farm.
- How about a historic connection to your region, like Steamboat Landing Herb Farm or Gold Rush Herb Gardens?
- Capitalize on something descriptive of your family partnership, like Three Sisters Herb Gardens or Molly 'n Me Herbs.

Make It Legal

Once you've decided on a name for your farm, you'll need to register it with your local government (city, county, or state) authorities. In doing so, you ascertain that no one else in your area is already using that name, ensure that no one else in your area can legally take on your business name at a later date, and give your company its first legal status. The latter is important because banks won't give you a business account without a fictitious business name statement, also called a dba (for "doing business as"). And without a business account, many suppliers won't deal with you.

Obtaining a dba is easy, although the process varies a bit in different regions of the country. In the state of Florida, for instance, you call the office of the Secretary of State and, after a hold period (generally long enough for one basil transplant to reach maturity) are given the opportunity to check on up to three potential business names. When

Herb Business Name Brainstorming

List three ideas based on your area's scenic, historic or weather features:

1. _____

2. _____

3. _____

List three ideas incorporating a family or partner theme:

1. _____

2. _____

3. _____

After you've decided which name you like best, have you:

❏ Tried it aloud to make sure it's easily understood and pronounced? (Has it passed muster with your family? Have you had a friend call to see how it sounds over the phone?)

❏ Checked your local Yellow Pages to make sure the same or similar name is not already listed?

❏ Checked with your local business name authority to make sure it's available?

Smart Tip

Tip...

While you're doing the local authority thing, apply for a business license. This generally consists of filling out a simple form and paying a nominal annual fee. It's simple, quick, and saves you from possible bureaucratic red tape later on if you're discovered to be doing business without it.

you hit on one that hasn't already been appropriated, the Secretary's office sends you a registration form. You mail back the completed form, the registration fee, and a form from your local newspaper verifying that you've advertised your dba for one week. In return, you receive your business name certificate, and *voilà*—your farm is official!

In other areas of the country, you might simply pop down to your city or county clerk's office, thumb through the roster of business names, and then complete the registration procedure at the clerk's window. To find out the procedure in your area, check in first with the county clerk's office or ask the commercial accounts officer at your bank.

Building a Framework

Another important element of your company's foundation is its legal structure. To keep the IRS happy, you must choose to operate as a sole proprietorship, a partnership, or a corporation, with variations thereon. Many herbal entrepreneurs go with the simplest and least expensive version, the sole proprietorship. You can always switch to

The Virtual Name

If you'll have a Web site, you'll need to register your business Web site name, or domain name, which is the www.whatever thing people type in to access your virtual farm. Like a dba, no two companies can have the same domain name, so you'll have to think up several versions of the name you want in case one's already been taken.

Here's what you do: Go into your Web browser and type in www.networksolutions.com. Now you're at the (surprise!) Network Solutions Web site, which is very user-friendly—and fun! Following the easy directions, check to see if the domain name you've chosen has been taken. If it has, choose another one. When you find a permutation that's available, register online. The cost—if you already have a Web host to handle your site—is $35 for a one-year registration, or $40 for a one-year reservation if you want to reserve a name, but you don't plan to use it right away.

Beware!

"If you're making a 'nutritional' product and want to get it into major chains," advises Maureen Rogers of the Herb Growing and Marketing Network, "you may be required to show proof of liability. That can run $2,000 to $4,000 per year, depending on the product and the amount of coverage you need."

another format later on if and when you take on partners and/or employees.

You might not think an herb farmer would need an on-call attorney—after all, you're not a Teflon don or insider-trading Wall Street hot shot. But as a businessperson, you should have a good attorney on call, one who understands both business and product law. You'll want him to check over any contracts you write with wholesalers and distributors and to advise you on the fine points of general small-business law while you're at it.

If you'll make and sell any sort of products—baby wash or bath oil to tinctures and teas and anything in between—you'll definitely want advice on local and national rules and regulations on what you can do to protect yourself against possible legal problems. (This is not something to manufacture worries about, but in an era of consumer-generated lawsuits for even the most frivolous of reasons, it's something to keep in mind.) You won't need to call your attorney often, but there's no point in waiting for a problem before establishing a relationship.

Along with that on-call attorney, you'll want to look into hiring an accountant to fill out those tax returns and advise you of any special ways you can save money with your business structure.

And don't forget your insurance agent! She can be an invaluable source of information and expertise. If your office will be in your home, you'll need to find out if your homeowners' package covers your business assets, inventory, and equipment, or if you need additional coverage. If you're based outside the home, you'll want coverage for these same items, as well as for your physical location.

Following the Rules

Besides the usual business rules, like getting a business permit and a dba, there are some special ones you may need to adhere to for your herbal products. "For selling anything other than plants, you may need an agricultural license, liability insurance, and/or retail license—there are lots of regulations," says Cindy M. of the Texas Herb Growers and Marketers Association. "You need to check with your state regulatory agencies when producing food-type or supplement products, such as tea, dried bulk herbs, herbal vinegars and oils, tinctures, etc., to see if you need a manufacturer's license and/or a certified kitchen."

And that's not all—at least not in some states. "In Texas," Cindy adds, "anytime you put anything into a container, be it dried rosemary or mint or fresh-cut parsley in

▲

Taxing Matters

Sales taxes are another legal element that varies with locale, but they must be collected on every sale you make. Before you start selling your herbs or products, you'll need to apply for a sales license or permit. Check with state and local authorities for the rules in your area. If you sell via mail order, you'll also need to collect sales tax for residents of some states—ask your accountant for the details that apply to you.

While a sales permit means more paperwork, it also has a secret bonus: Once you get one, you no longer have to pay sales tax on materials, merchandise, or supplies you buy wholesale for resale to your customers.

plastic clamshell, you need a manufacturer's license and a certified kitchen. To sell bunches of fresh or dried herbs, you do not need licensing—it falls under the category of produce."

If you'll run a tearoom, restaurant, or other operation that could be considered food-related, or stay up late at home mixing edibles (which can include teas, tinctures, and anything else ingestible) to sell, you'll need to check in with your local health department or department of agriculture. Most states prohibit selling goods cooked up in a home kitchen unless it's been specially modified for commercial use.

"Our food products are all certified organic, so we're inspected by the state agriculture department," says Mike R., the lavender grower in Sequim, Washington. The department administers both surprise and advance warning inspections, monitoring storage techniques, labeling, and processing.

"The organic certification is quite a process," Mike explains, "and includes inspections and application fees. It's jumping through hoops, but it's no big deal. They give us good guidelines and maintain a good monitoring program."

Some states regulate the intrastate sale of potted plants and demand a nursery sanitation certificate, advises Maureen Rogers of the Herb Growing and Marketing Network. Most states, however, have no regulations for agricultural products sold on farm sites or through local farmers' markets. To make sure you're on the up-and-up in your area, check in with your local department of agriculture.

An Office of Your Own

Even though you'll spend much of your time among your herbs, you'll need an office in which to deal with paperwork, work on marketing campaigns, and handle Web site and mail orders. But one of the perks of being an herb farmer is that you can have a home office. No more commuting miles to sit behind some other boss's desk, and no more giving your lunch money to fast-food emporiums.

You can set up your office work space anywhere in the house or barn that's convenient. If you'll set up in your home, you should have a dedicated office, a room that's reserved just for the business. You can locate this room in a den, a FROG (finished room over garage), the garage itself, or a spare bedroom. Keep in mind that whatever space you choose will be your work station and command center.

Smart Tip
Wise farmers and gardeners keep annual journals detailing where and when each botanical was planted in the field or bed and how it performed, as well as noting weather and other variables. This helps determine what next year's crops will be—and where they'll go.

If a dedicated office is not an option for you, you can also station yourself in a corner of the kitchen or at the dining room table. If you've got a noisy family, however, a cubbyhole in your bedroom is liable to be much more conducive to quiet, clear thinking than a nook in the family room with the television blaring at all hours.

The Big Write-Off

A big advantage to the home office is the ability to wear two hats—to be at home with your family and be at work at the same time. Another advantage is the ability to count your home office as a tax write-off. The IRS will graciously allow you to deduct money from your income taxes if you're using a portion of your home as your income-producing work space. You can deduct a percentage of expenses equivalent to the percentage of space your home office occupies. If, for example, you're using one room in an eight-room house, you can deduct one-eighth of your rent or mortgage plus one-eighth of your utility bills.

There is, of course, an "if" involved here. You can only claim this deduction if you're using the space solely as your office. If you've turned your spare bedroom into your office and you don't use it for anything but conducting your business, then you qualify. But if you've appropriated a corner of the living room for your office and you've still got the television and the kids' toys all over the room, you may have a hard time convincing the IRS the room's sole function is as a business work space.

Organizational Issues

Even though you may be checking your e-mail in your blue (or green) jeans in between thinning seedlings, it's important to remember that you're still a professional. Your work quarters, like you, should be organized and efficient.

Appropriate a desk or table large enough to hold your computer, keyboard, phone, pencil holder, stapler, etc., and still have enough room left to spread out your working papers.

Make sure you have enough space to neatly file contracts, invoices, and order forms; stash catalogs and brochures from suppliers; and store all those herbal books and trade

The Herb Office

Use this handy worksheet to locate and design your home office.

Start by listing three possible locations in your home for your office, which should include a work area for you and enough space for your desk, computer, and telephone:

1. _____

2. _____

3. _____

Make a physical survey of each location:

❑ Are phone and electrical outlets placed so that your equipment can easily access them? Or will you be faced with unsightly, unsafe cords snaking across the carpet?

❑ Measure your space. Will your current desk or table (or the one you have your eye on) fit?

❑ Do you have adequate lighting? If not, can you create or import it?

❑ Is there proper ventilation?

❑ What is the noise factor?

❑ Is there room to spread out your work?

❑ Optional: How close is it to the coffee maker? Refrigerator? (This can be either a plus or minus, depending on your current waistline and jitter factor.)

❑ Take a survey of your possible home-assembly and packing spaces. Is there adequate lighting, ventilation, and work space? What is the humidity factor? Will you need to construct special shelving or add other storage space? If so, make notes here:

_____

_____

Fun Fact

The market for herbal soaps and bath products is bigger than ever. A recent Gallup poll revealed that 75 percent of Americans bathe daily during winter. In a similar poll taken in 1950, only 29 percent of Americans said they bathed every winter day.

publications. It's OK to start off with cardboard file boxes purchased from the office supply store or even produce boxes scrounged from the local market. But keep in mind that you must be able to access your files quickly and easily. It's no fun digging through the back of the linen closet or rummaging through unwieldy stacks of papers every time somebody calls with a question.

If you'll sell products, you'll need to consider creating an area in which you'll store, assemble and pack them for shipping. This can be the barn, your garage or attic, or a spare bedroom. The main criteria is that it's clean, well-lit, low in humidity and has adequate work surfaces.

Setting Up Shop

For many herbal entrepreneurs, a cozy and fragrant shop, literally stuffed to the rafters with fragrant botanicals and spilling over with books, cards, garden tools, and container plants, is as powerful a dream as the herb farm or garden. But while the ideal herb shop looks charmingly haphazard, a lot of thought and planning should go into its design and layout.

An herb shop can occupy just about any space you choose, so long as customers will make the trip and zoning laws don't prohibit retail activity. But whether you set up operations in a lofty barn, a tiny drying shed, or an actual storefront, you'll want to follow some planning guidelines.

Divide and Conquer

Working from the entrance to the back wall of your proposed location, imagine your space divided into thirds. Devote the first third, the one closest to the front door, to the products you think will sell best. This might seem counterintuitive—why wouldn't you put the bestsellers in the back so customers have to stroll past everything else to reach them? The answer is that hot products, whether glimpsed through a storefront window or open door, draw people in. Once you've caught customers' attention, they'll

Smart Tip

Tip...

Don't forget to spotlight seasonal merchandise. From plant starters and topiaries to teddy bears and decorations, holiday-themed wares draw customers in.

Tip...

Smart Tip

Carefully consider aisle space. You want enough room between displays for customers to maneuver with ease but not so much that you sacrifice merchandising space.

walk in, look around, and move toward the back in search of other fascinating discoveries. But if you don't catch them right up front, you lose them, and they'll take their interest—and their pocketbooks—someplace else. So set out your fairy houses, bird motels, potpourri nestled in faux birds nests, seasonal wreaths, or other popular products right up front.

Set your next bestsellers in the middle third of the shop and your least profitable products in the very back. This "back room" could include crafting supplies from ribbons to wreath forms, a display devoted to sale merchandise (stuff that hasn't really sold up front and needs to go), garden tools and seeds—or unrelated products.

You'll also want to mentally divide your store into three horizontal levels: above the head, at eye level and from the shoulders down. From a distance, above-the-head merchandise, banners or other objects should draw customers into the shop. Once they're inside, upper-level merchandising continues to draw people in and toward the back, while eye level and lower products work to keep their interest.

Keep in mind that most people don't really look down unless they're searching supermarket shelves for the only brand of cereal Junior will eat. Use shelves, tables, cases, and other display surfaces to put as much as possible between waist and eye level.

Most people think of "merchandise" as a noun to describe a store's wares. But it's also a verb, and an important one. The manner in which you display, or merchandise, your products can make the crucial difference between a successful operation and one that sinks into the dead zone.

Shops that lay out all their wares on a single plane, either slammed against the walls on racks or set out on tables like a sort of permanent garage sale, are boring. They don't elicit customer interest. Experiment with different display pieces. Take an old bedroom dresser; scatter bath and beauty products across the top, then open the drawers slightly and allow dried botanicals, sachets, and herb-motif T-shirts or tea towels to spill out. Stack pieces of elderly luggage two or three high and use them, opened, to display merchandise. Use a kitchen or dining room sideboard to display herbal jellies, vinegars, and tea blends. Fasten an old bicycle against a wall and fill its basket with stuffed animals. The more imaginative your displays, the more customers will stay and shop.

Fun Fact

According to a recent study by Simmons Market Research Bureau, people in the 35- to 44-year age range purchase more gardening products via mail order than any other age group.

Retail shops can generally count on two types of customers: destination traffic, customers who already know what they want and make a beeline for it, and shopping traffic, people who are "just looking" and may or may not purchase anything. Shopping traffic customers usually meander through a store, alighting at whatever catches their fancy. But they also tend to drift to the right from the front door, which means that destination shoppers tend to move to the left to avoid the crowds.

These traffic patterns provide a terrific key to the layout of your shop. You can place wares that repeat customers come in for often, from crafting supplies and potpourri refresher oils to skin lotions, on the left side of your shop. Put the impulse-buy, "just looking" stuff on the right where meanderers can browse to their heart's content.

Employees Only

Whether your shop is in an historic building, an uptown shopping plaza or your own backyard, you'll need a space just for you and your employees, that back room with the closed door behind which customers dare not tread. What's in there?

As much as will fit, including:

- *Storage space.* You'll use this space for extra stock, damaged items waiting to be returned to wholesalers, extra gift wrapping and packaging materials, the crock pot for serving herb-mulled cider at Christmas, and whatever else won't fit under the counter up front.

- *A file cabinet or two for invoices and receipts.* If you have room, you may even want to organize a small office with the same basic setup as your home office. Remember that whether in a home or commercial space, your computer should occupy a place of honor, away from dirt, drafts and blinding sunlight. Ditto for your printer and fax machine. And don't forget every office's icon—the coffee maker!

- *Shipping and assembly areas.* If you'll assemble products to sell or ship, you'll need adequately lit work surfaces on which to prepare your wares.

7

Sowing the Seeds
General Start-Up Costs

One of the terrific things about the herb business is that it can be a fairly inexpensive start-up, especially if you've already got land to grow on. But, as with any new business, there are costs involved.

▲

Your start-up expenses will fall into three basic categories:

- Routine office expenses that you'll incur whether you go wholesale or retail: These are things like a computer, software, a business telephone line, and membership fees to trade organizations.

- Herb growing and herbal merchandise production expenses that will vary with the size of your farm, your growing methods, and your products: These are items like irrigation, greenhouses, drying sheds, plant pots and markers, and farm equipment.

- Sales and promotion expenses, which include items like price tags, labels, ribbons and wrappings, cash register, and displays.

We'll explore each of these categories in a separate chapter, with this one devoted to office expenses.

Does Compute

Perhaps the most important office item on your start-up list is a computer system—a hard drive, monitor, mouse, modem, and printer, plus whatever peripherals you choose to tack on. With a good system as your farm office manager, you can easily—and professionally—tackle any number of business tasks, including:

- Performing accounting functions and generating financial reports

- Creating your own brochures, display ads, and other direct-mail pieces

- Generating invoices and order forms

- Maintaining customer databases

- Accessing research materials and other business resources online

- Selling via an online brochure or catalog

- Communicating with repeat and potential customers, suppliers, and distributors via e-mail

Your new computer should be a Pentium-class with a current version of the Windows operating system since this is what all but the most antiquated garage-sale software packages are geared for. To run your software properly, you'll need at least 64MB RAM, plus at least an 8GB to 10GB hard drive, a 24X or better CD-ROM drive, and a 56 KBps modem. You can expect to pay from $2,000 to $4,000 for a good name-brand computer, with prices increasing as you add on goodies.

> **Tip...**
>
> ## Smart Tip
> Monitors are often sold separately. You'll want an SVGA high-resolution color display and a screen large enough to make long-term viewing comfortable, say 17 inches or more. Remember that a few extra dollars spent upfront will save hours of squinting in the long haul. You can expect to dish out $300 to $400 for a solid, midrange model.

Software Smarts

As great an office mate as your computer can be, it can't help you unless you give it software to make it sing. A stunning array of software lines the shelves of most office supply stores, ready to help you perform every business task—design and print your own checks, develop professional-quality marketing materials, make mailing lists and labels, even act as your own attorney and accountant.

Most new computers come preloaded with all the software you'll need for basic office procedures. If it doesn't come already equipped with the following programs, shop till you drop for versions you like, then load them up:

- *Word processing*, with which you can dash off correspondence, contracts, seminar or workshop course materials, press releases, and articles. You can even write your own cookbook or herbal to sell! A good basic program such as Microsoft Word or Corel WordPerfect can be had for $85 to $220.

- *Accounting*, like QuickBooks or Microsoft Money to track your business finances. Virtual checkbooks, these programs allow you to track income and expenses, print out all sorts of financial reports and even write checks. Expect to pay $80 to $250 for your cyberspace accountant.

- *Desktop publishing*, which you can use to create recipes, hang tags, labels, cards, brochures, fliers, and all sorts of other sales and promotional materials. Two good choices are Bröderbund's Print Shop Deluxe, which tallies in at about $50, or Microsoft Publisher 2000, which goes for about $100.

- *For those mailing lists* you'll develop of past and potential customers, you'll also want to purchase a list management program like Parsons Technology's Ultimate Mail Manager—which includes U.S. Postal Service-certified technology for ZIP code accuracy—for about $60.

In the Mail

If you plan on selling by mail order, a postage meter may keep you from going postal. Depending on how spiffy you choose to go from among the various models available, you can not only stamp your mail but fold, staple, insert, seal, label, weigh, sort, stack, and wrap it. And, where you once had to lug your postage meter down to the post office and stand in line to get it reset, you don't anymore! Now you simply reset via phone or computer.

The fancier and faster the machine, the more expensive it will be to rent, lease or purchase. As a ballpark figure, you can expect to rent a postage meter/electronic scale combo for about $30 per month and up.

Caught in the Web

A safe and reliable ISP, or Internet service provider, like America Online or EarthLink is a must. With the power of the World Wide Web at your command, you can go anywhere on the globe instantly. On the Web you can search and sell your herbs and products, communicate with customers and vendors, even get detailed maps to other herb farms, and make airline and hotel reservations for trade shows and conferences. And it's cheap! Most ISPs charge about $20 to $25 per month and give you unlimited Web and e-mail access.

If you plan to sell by mail order (which includes Internet sales), a Web site can be a boon to your business. Even if you don't go mail order, a Web site can help promote your products to both wholesale and retail customers.

The cost of putting up and maintaining a business site varies considerably. If you're lucky enough to have a computer brain in the family, or if you take the time to become your own computer expert, you can pencil in a zero under Web site design and construction costs. But if you outsource your Web site construction, you should ink in about $300 to $500 for hands-on help from a Web site designer. Or, as a third option, find a friend who'll put up your site in exchange for lawn mowing, babysitting, or a steady supply of fresh herbs.

Computer Extras

If you plan to produce your own Web site or your own advertising materials (or both), you might want to spring for a digital camera. With one of these gadgets, you simply snap photos of your herbs or herbal products, then connect the camera to your computer and click a few icons with your mouse—and you've got virtual herbs right in your desktop publishing program! Expect to pay $400 to $700 for a good-quality digital camera.

You may also want to consider a scanner, a keen gadget that imports, or "pastes," graphics from just about any printed medium—books, photographs, brochures, or original art, for example—into your desktop publishing program. You can pick up a print-quality scanner for about $150 to $400.

A good printer is a must. You'll have promotional materials, order forms, mailing labels, contracts, invoices, and sundry other materials, and they all need to look polished and professional. Purchase an inkjet capable of producing every conceivable color as well as black and white for $250 to $500.

> ## ⚠ Beware!
> Remember that you can't use anything somebody else holds a copyright on, including graphics, artworks, and text. Make sure the material you scan into your own work is copyright-free, or in the case of another company's brochures, that you have permission to use the material before you import it.

Dial Tone

Now that just about everybody communicates by e-mail, a fax machine is not a hard-and-fast necessity. But it's a nice touch. Customers who can't—or won't—order products on the Internet can fax their orders to you. And you can send and receive seminar or workshop materials, invoices, or anything else on a printed or handwritten page.

If you want just the fax, you can purchase a basic plain-paper model for as little as $100. A fancy multifunction machine runs up to $800.

We assume that you already have a telephone, in which case you already know all about phone bills. As a professional herb entrepreneur, however, you'll need more on the phone front. You should have two separate dedicated lines for your business: one for handling phone calls and another for your fax machine and ISP. If you've ever tried to call a friend who's got his phone line tied up surfing the Net, you'll know how important this is. And as a businessperson, you can't let phone calls go unanswered—it's unprofessional and results in lost orders. If customers can't reach you, they give up.

Costs vary depending on the number of features you add to your telephone service and which local and long-distance carriers you go with, but for the purposes of start-up budgeting, allocate about $25 per line. You'll also need to add the phone company's installation fee, which should be in the range of $40 to $60. Check with your local phone company to determine exactly what these costs are in your area.

If your office will be in your home, go for a two-line phone—you can have your office line on one and your home line on the other with that ultraprofessional hold button to switch between calls if necessary. (Just don't forget which line's which. It's not cool to pick up the business line and launch into a tirade about tattoos, only to dis-

---

The Message Taker

Since you'll probably start off solo, you'll need somebody to answer the phone while you're out working in the garden or greenhouse, delivering orders or hosting workshops. You'll need an electronic secretary in the form of voice mail, which is the phone company's answer to the answering machine.

Like an answering machine, voice mail takes your messages when you're not in the office. If you have call waiting, and you choose not to answer that second call, voice mail will take a message for you. With voice mail, as with many answering machines, you can access your messages from a remote location.

Voice mail costs depend on your local Ma Bell and the features you choose, but you can expect to pay in the range of $6 to $20 a month.

▲

cover it's your best customer on the other end and not your teenage daughter.) If you need to answer the third line coming into your home—the one for your fax and ISP—you can pick up the handset on the fax machine.

A speaker is a nice feature for your two-line phone, especially for all those on-hold-forever calls to your banker, attorney, insurance company or whoever. Your hands are free to do other tasks, and your ear won't go numb listening to instrumental versions of Beatles hits. Expect to pay about $70 to $150 for a two-line speakerphone with auto redial, memory dial, flashing lights, mute button, and other assorted goodies.

Powered Up

For those periodic power outages, you'll want to invest in a UPS, or uninterruptible power supply (not to be confused with UPS, the delivery company), for your computer system, especially if you live in an area where lightning or power surges are common.

You may not realize that even a flicker of power loss can shut down your computer, causing it to forget all the data you've carefully entered during your current work session, or—horrors—fry your computer's brains entirely. With a UPS, however, you won't lose power to your system when the house power fails or flickers. Instead, the unit flashes red and sounds a warning, giving you ample time to safely shut down.

If you'll be spending a lot of time on the Internet, be sure that your UPS includes phone line protection. Expect to pay $125 and up.

Equally important, a surge protector safeguards your electronic equipment from power spikes during storms or outages. Your battery backup will double as a surge protector for your computer hard drive and monitor, but you'll want protection for those other valuable office allies: your printer, fax machine, and copier. They don't need a battery backup because no data will be lost if the power goes out, and a surge protector does the job for a lot less money. If you've got a fax machine, be sure the surge protector also defends its phone line. Expect to pay in the range of $15 to $60 for a surge protector.

Tip...

Smart Tip

The copier is an optional item, but as you grow, you may find it a necessary luxury for running off forms, fliers, and other goodies. It's far easier to run off one copy or 50 in your own office than to have to run down to the copy center every time the need arises. Copiers range from $400 to $800 and up.

Taking Credit

If you plan on Internet or retail sales, you'll want an electronic credit card terminal so you can take payments online. It's faster and easier for customers and for you because you can take credit card information over the phone, on the Web, or by fax, and send orders immediately.

More and more merchant card service firms are springing up that cater specifically to small-business owners and Internet entrepreneurs. Shop around (especially on the Web), and you'll find a variety to choose from.

What can you expect to pay for an electronic terminal? Fees depend on several factors, including the company you go with and your personal credit history. Keep in mind that this is an industry that's growing rapidly with better deals all the time. You can lease or purchase the terminal itself from the merchant bank, or you can buy a used (but still serviceable) machine from a company that's gone out of business or has upgraded its unit.

All the Trimmings

Office furniture is optional. Naturally, you need something to sit on and to hold your computer equipment and files, but if you're homebased, it's perfectly acceptable to start off with an old door set on cinder blocks for a desk, a cast-off kitchen chair, and a former lettuce box for your files. As your business—and your profits—grow, buy the professional stuff.

If you choose to start with the real thing, expect to find midrange desks from $200 to $300, computer work centers for $200, chairs from $60 to $250, printer stands from $50 to $75, two-drawer letter-sized file cabinets (which can double as your printer stand) from $25 to $100, and four-shelf book-cases for $70.

Your computer and printer won't do much good without paper on which to process your work. You'll also need to round out your own office supplies with stationery, envelopes, and business cards; pens and pencils; and all those miscellaneous bits like paper clips, tape, and staples. If you'll do any sort of mail order (which includes Internet sales), you'll want shipping materials in which to send off your products.

> **Tip...**
>
> **Smart Tip**
> Even though your computer probably has an on-board calculator program, you'll want to have the real thing close at hand. You can do quick calculations without complex mouse maneuvers, and with the paper tape, you can check your work. Expect to pay under $15 for a battery-operated model and $25 to $75 for a plug-in job.

Plan on allocating about $25 to $50 for a box of good-quality printer/copier paper, which will give you 10 reams of 500 sheets each. You'll spend in the range of $200 to $400 for stationery, printed at a quick-stop place like Kinko's, and $150 for a starter collection of shipping supplies, including sealing tape and a gun-style tape dispenser.

Members Only

We've now given you a shopping list of every item for the well-equipped herb farm office—including two take-along checklists to have in hand when you hit the office and computer superstores. (You'll find them on pages 90 and 91.)

But there's more. Don't forget to budget for membership in professional organizations. Besides help in starting and growing your business, these groups give you discounts on all sorts of business services, help you stay up to speed on industry issues and events, and act as your voice in legislative affairs.

"The one thing I can't stress too much is the benefit of contacts with others in the field," says Cindy M. of the Texas Herb Growers and Marketers Association. "Whether it be to find new outlets for wholesalers or for retailers to find new products, or just to discuss the problems encountered in the day-to-day running of a business, being a part of THGMA makes running a business easier."

The Herb Growing and Marketing Network goes all the way for you, providing you with these perks:

- A reading list designed for your herb business
- Information about everything from government regulations to accounting
- Contacts with potential customers
- Free classified ads in the network's trade publication and on its Web site
- A listing in the print and online versions of the *Herbal Green Pages*, a top industry resource guide
- Reduced rates on liability insurance, phone service, and employee health care

The price for all this and more is just $95 per year.

The International Herb Association is also well worth joining. With a goal of encouraging herbal entrepreneurs, the group offers members:

> ## Fun Fact
>
> When the group of herb professionals that later became the International Herb Association first met in Lebanon, Ohio, in 1985, they expected a modest turnout of about 25 herbal souls. To their astonishment, 92 people from seven states, representing 56 different businesses, showed up.

- Access to herb professionals around the globe
- Information on everything from packaging, labeling, design, and display to taxes and stress management
- Your own Web site designed and put up by a professional webmaster at a discounted fee

The annual fee to join is $100.

Add It Up

OK, now it's time to don your bookkeeping cap and tally up the company setup expenses we've investigated in this chapter. Besides the ones we've already checked into, you'll want to add other expenses like business licenses, business insurance, legal advice, and all the other costs intrinsic to any company's birth. And don't forget to throw a grand opening garden party!

To give you an idea of how much you can expect to budget, see page 92 to check out the company setup costs for two hypothetical herb businesses, Sage Advice Herb Farm and Herban Planet. Sage Advice, located on a country acre that's a part of the owner's home site, will sell potted herbs to tourists in the area as well as via mail order. Herban Planet, working from a once-abandoned half-acre city lot, will market fresh-cut herbs to local restaurants and specialty markets as well as make and sell herb crafts like soaps and wreaths.

Both companies will operate a home office with the owner as the sole employee. Sage Advice's owner already has a computer system and software and doesn't plan to upgrade immediately, but Herban Planet will start off with all-new, top-of-the-line equipment.

Use the worksheet on page 93 to list your own company setup costs. If you copy a couple of extra sheets, you can work up several options, compare them all, and decide which will be the best for you.

▲

The Herb Farmer's Office Equipment Checklist

Use this handy list as a shopping guide for equipping your office. It's been designed with the one-person home office in mind, so if you've got partners or employees, or you just won $250,000 in merchandise from an office supplies superstore, you may want to make modifications.

After you've finished your shopping, fill in the purchase price next to each item, add up the total, and use this figure in the "Company Setup Costs" worksheet on page 93.

Current Windows-based Pentium-class PC with SVGA monitor, modem, and CD-ROM	$ _____
Inkjet printer	_____
Fax machine	_____
Software	
Word processing	_____
Desktop publishing	_____
Accounting	_____
Mailing list management	_____
Phones, two to three lines	_____
Voice mail	_____
Uninterruptible power supply	_____
Surge protector	_____
Calculator	_____
Office supplies (see minilist)	_____
Not on the critical list	
Digital camera	_____
Scanner	_____
Copier	_____
Desk	_____
Desk chair	_____
Filing cabinet	_____
Bookcase	_____
Total Office Equipment and Furniture Expenditures	$ _____

The Office Supplies Mini-Shopping List

Computer/copier/fax paper $ _____

Blank business cards   _____

Blank letterhead stationery   _____

Matching envelopes   _____

Mail order shipping materials:

  Bubble-lined envelopes   _____

  Sealing tape   _____

  Tape dispenser   _____

File folders   _____

Return address stamp or stickers   _____

Extra printer cartridge   _____

Mousepad   _____

Miscellaneous office supplies (pencils, paper clips, etc.)   _____

Extra fax cartridge   _____

Total Office Supplies Expenditures $ _____

Company Setup Costs for Hypothetical Business

Costs	Sage Advice	Herban Planet
Professional associations	$95	$195
Equipment expenses	1,607	5,005
Licenses	100	100
Phone	90	90
Magazine subscriptions	42	42
Grand opening	100	300
Legal services	375	375
Miscellaneous postage	50	50
Internet service	20	20
Web site design and marketing	0	500
Insurance	500	500
Subtotal	2,979	7,177
Miscellaneous expenses (Add 10 percent of total)	297	717
Total Setup Costs	**$3,276**	**$7,894**

Company Setup Costs

Professional associations $ _____

Office equipment (see worksheet on page 90)   _____

Licenses   _____

Phone   _____

Magazine subscriptions   _____

Grand opening   _____

Legal services   _____

Internet service provider   _____

Web site design and marketing   _____

Stationery/Office supplies   _____

Insurance   _____

Subtotal   _____

Miscellaneous expenses
  (Add roughly 10 percent of total)   _____

Your Total Setup Costs: _____

Fertilizing the Soil
Farming Start-Up Costs

In the last chapter we explored the expenses involved in setting up your business office, including a range of items from computer equipment to membership in professional organizations. But there's much more to the joy—and the cost—of herb farming. There is also all the nitty-gritty, get-your-hands-dirty, fun stuff particular to herb farming like soil, seeds, pots, and even bugs. And that's what we'll investigate in this chapter.

Down and Dirty

The most fundamental item you'll need for your herb farm is dirt, or, more properly, soil. You probably already have soil underfoot, but it may need amendments from sand to compost. And if you'll grow in pots or in raised beds, you'll have to get soil from somewhere to fill them, unless of course you choose to go with soilless mediums like perlite and peat moss. Prices will vary depending on the amendments or ingredients you choose as well as whether you buy a premixed medium. Here are some sample prices:

- *Perlite growing medium, 8 quart* $3
- *Potting soil, 2.5 cubic feet* $8
- *Sand, 40 pounds* $4
- *Mushroom compost, 40 pounds* $3

Whether you're preparing from scratch or reworking your land after a long winter's nap, you'll need to get your soil ready for planting—which means getting in there and plowing it with either hand tools or a rotary tiller. Rototillers, which are powered with gas instead of elbow grease, will run you about $600 to $1,000.

Even if you purchase the rototiller, you'll still want to stock a selection of hand tools such as the following:

- *Spading fork, spade, and trowel* $3 to $7 each
- *Shovel* $8 to $31
- *Hoe* $5 to $20
- *Pitchfork* $20 to $35
- *Cultivator* $9 to $20
- *Rake* $5 to $20
- *Pruning shears* $6 to $30

Don't forget the wheelbarrow for toting off all those piles of weeds, rocks, and assorted garden debris. Choose a snazzy 8-cubic-foot-capacity two-wheeled model for $100, a 6-cubic-foot steel one-wheeler for about $70, or the serviceable plastic one-wheeler for $25.

The Greenhouse Effect

A greenhouse is a terrific way to extend your growing season and to protect your precious herbs from the elements. Because you can place plants on shelves and benches and in hanging containers, you also get a lot more growing room for the square footage. And in nongrowing months, the greenhouse can be transformed into a drying shed.

As a start-up herb farmer, you'll probably want to go with a fairly small greenhouse and graduate to a larger size as your business grows—no need to purchase the 12,000-square-foot mansion immediately. There are several styles to choose from, from the funky but durable Quonset style to a more conventional gabled roof with a Dutch or French door. The more "designer" you go, the higher the price. Some greenhouses are constructed of PVC pipe, while others are hybrids made with redwood frames. Coverings range from 3.5-millimeter plastic (your basic trash bag material but heavier) to state-of-the-art honeycombed polyethylene panels. You can purchase special insulated flooring or make your own of brick or gravel.

Expect to spend anywhere from $500 for a basic 8½-foot-by-10-foot plastic-covered PVC model to $12,600 for a fancy 16-foot-by-36-foot aluminum-framed model with polycarbonate panels, a prehung glass storm door, and automatic ventilation system. If you're so inclined, you can also build a greenhouse to your own specifications and save significantly on costs. (Since even "ready-made" greenhouses come as kits you assemble at home, building your own isn't much different.)

Barbie's First Greenhouse

Just like with the Barbie or GI Joe doll you had as a kid, once you've got a greenhouse, you'll suddenly find you've got to buy all sorts of accessories to go with it. Shade cloth, flooring, exhaust fans, heaters, thermostatically controlled vents, drip irrigation systems, misting systems on timers... the list goes on and on.

For a newbie with a small greenhouse, it's not necessary to buy every fancy gadget immediately. You may do just fine with a watering can for irrigation and a kitchen timer to remind you to go out there and open the vents on sunny afternoons and

Dollar Stretcher
Fill five-gallon covered black buckets with water and set them in your greenhouse for those cold winter nights. The water will heat up during the day and release solar heat at night.

shut them again in the evening. Or you may determine that in your part of the country or with your schedule, some of these items are necessities. The best idea is to do your homework; then let your lifestyle, your specific site requirements, and your pocketbook be your guide.

To give you an idea of costs for some of these accessories, take a look at the following list:

- *12-inch exhaust fan with thermostat* — $200
- *8-inch circulation fan* — $108
- *1,000-cfm (cubic feet per minute) to 1,600-cfm circulation fan designed for attics* — $39 to $78
- *Solar-powered vent opener* — $46
- *Shade cloth* — $4 to $6 per feet
- *Natural gas or propane heater* — $425
- *Drip or mist irrigation system* — $30 to $50
- *Programmable water timer* — $40 to $54
- *Halide grow light and track* — $440
- *Mat flooring* — $5 per feet
- *Seedling heat mat* — $23 to $65
- *Lumber for benches and shelves* — $8 per board
- *Cinder block for bench bases* — $1 each

These are sample costs only; prices may be higher or lower, depending on your supplier and the quality of the products. To save more start-up funds, you can improvise by using, for example, Astroturf instead of custom flooring, or an attic fan for ventilation instead of a greenhouse fan. Growers report varying results with these substitutes, so experiment and see what works for you.

Smart Tip

Tip...

Make sure your greenhouse panels or coverings are UV protected—preferably embedded and not coated. This will extend the life of your greenhouse.

Water, Water Everywhere

You'll water by hand or with drip or mist irrigation in the greenhouse. But what about in your fields or garden? You can't easily water a half acre or more with your trusty watering can. Your options include overhead watering with an inexpensive plastic sprinkler, the good-old Rainbird-type system of connected sprinklers, or the methods of choice for most herb farmers—ooze or drip irrigation.

Ooze irrigation uses a porous hose of funky recycled rubber that, as the name implies, oozes water along its length. The drip method employs high-tech poly tubing studded with drip or bubble nozzles and misters. Because they deliver water at the root level instead of spewing it indiscriminately like sprinklers, drip and ooze systems use water more efficiently—resulting in a more manageable water bill. There's no splashed mud that you'll have to wash off before delivering your herbs to customers. And if you turn off the misters, you get another bonus: reduced possibility of fungus growth or sunburn on wet foliage. You save on damaged plants and utility bills and do your part toward water conservation.

Expect to pay about $10 for 75 feet of ooze hose and about $300 and up for a drip system. Or start off low-budget (and low-tech) with a plain garden hose (100 feet for $15 to $32) and a watering wand (about $3) or a sprinkler soaker hose—which is your basic garden hose punched with holes—that goes for about $8 for 50 feet.

Dollar Stretcher

Improvise! Use less expensive plywood instead of lumber for greenhouse benches.

A Seedy Story

Seeds go for anywhere from $1.25 a packet (generally 50 to 200 seeds) to $8 per ounce, although some can go as high as $225 per ounce. If you think that's exorbitant, consider that you get as many as 88,000 seeds in 1 ounce—far more than you're likely to need as a start-up farmer. And gold standard prices are not the norm; most seeds are reasonably priced at $1.50 to $3 per packet.

Also consider that many herbs can be grown from cuttings and division. Once you start your first plants, you can "make" your own new plants year after year without buying new seeds. And you can also harvest your own seeds from some herbs instead of buying new the next year.

Some herbs—French tarragon is a notable example here—cannot be grown from seeds, so you'll need to purchase cuttings to start in your garden. Plan on a per-plant cost of $2 to $5, depending on what you buy; whether it's a plug, a liner or a plant; and where you purchase it. (Mail order plants tend to be more expensive than those purchased at a garden center.) *Plugs* are very small starter plants that don't yet have an established root system; when you purchase them as perennials, they often come in a dormant state. *Liners* are still babies, but one size up from plugs.

For starting seeds in the greenhouse and for selling potted plants, you'll need potting materials. Look for plug trays and propagation trays for 75 cents to 80 cents each. The most popular sizes of plastic pots—the norm at garden centers everywhere—are 3, 4, and 6 inches. Expect to pay in the range of $40 to $80 for 400 to 1,000 pots, depending on size and quantity ordered.

Inexpensive plastic pot stakes for labeling your herbs range in price from $14 to $17 per thousand, depending on size. Or go fancy—and more expensive—with T-shaped stakes that run about $30 per 100 units.

Herbs on Wheels

If you plan to deliver your herbs to customers, you'll definitely need a set of wheels. Depending on your volume, you may be able to start off with your current jalopy. But sooner or later, you'll need to move up to a van or pickup truck into which you can load trays of pots, buckets of fresh foliage, or baskets and bags of fresh-cut greens. A pickup—the quintessential farm workhorse—is also a boon for hauling soil amendments, fertilizers, and other bulky and dirty materials.

If you already have a vehicle, you may have the wheels problem licked. If not, you'll have to go auto shopping. How much you pay for a vehicle will depend on whether you

Black Gold

To the farmer, black gold isn't oil—it's compost. It's also cheap (as in free), fun to make, and earth-friendly. If you haven't been reading *Organic Gardening* or *Mother Earth News* since those heady back-to-nature days of the 1970s and aren't familiar with compost, here's the scoop: Compost is simply organic vegetable waste—leaves and flowers from the garden and orange peelings, limp lettuce, and eggshells from the kitchen. You rake it all into a big pile and then turn it once a day with a garden fork or shovel. Faster than you might believe possible, this yuck magically decomposes into exquisitely healthy loam.

You can devise a compost pile in a corner of your backyard and turn it at regular intervals with the liberal application of elbow grease and hand tools, or you can purchase various ready-made compost bins, from a simple wire cube to a three-tiered affair powered by earthworms. Plan to spend from $35 to $100.

buy a new or preowned vehicle, a small truck or a full-sized one, and a bare-bones version or one loaded with optional features, like CD players and leather seats. You should plan on spending anywhere from $5,000 to $25,000.

Little Necessities

Smart Tip

Tip...

Keep your company wheels clean and tidy: A dirty vehicle is a poor reflection on your herb farm and your products. And don't forget to put your farm name on the sides! Expect to pay $25 to $500 for lettering and logo, depending on the size and complexity of your mobile signage.

You can bundle fresh-cut herbs with rubber bands; package them up in clamshells, those nifty clear plastic boxes you see in supermarkets everywhere; or stash them in plastic poly bags. (Make sure any packaging meets FDA approval.) Expect to pay about $55 per 500 herb-bundle-sized clamshells and $14 to $33 per case of 1,000 bags. Add $17 to $29 for a box of 5,000 pressure-sensitive labels that you can mark with rubber stamps or $17 to $18 for 1,000 to 2,000 laser printer labels.

If you plan to make and sell herb crafts—anything from sachets and soaps to wreaths—you'll probably have to purchase various supplies to turn them into reality. These may include glue; florist's tape; Oasis, or florist's foam; wire forms; and jars, bottles, and essential oils. How much you'll spend, of course, depends on what products you'll make and what techniques you'll use.

Your costs also depend on how wisely you shop. It's always better to buy supplies wholesale than retail, but it's also important to shop around. Prices can vary greatly

Spending Smart

Your start-up expenses need not be astronomical, just wisely allocated. "My start-up expenses were very small," says herb farmer Cindy M. in Hallettsville, Texas. "I spent under $5,000 total, and that included a small (10-foot-by-30-foot) greenhouse, some starter plants, seeds, plug trays, pots, trays, and planting medium. It also included magazine subscriptions, books, dues, and travel to conferences that first year."

"The greenhouses were probably the most expensive," Michele B. in Soddy Daisy, Tennessee, says of her farm's start-up expenses. "I'd say we spent close to $10,000 getting the business where it is right now. That includes a computer with extra phone line, printer, fax machine, credit card machine, greenhouses, shade cloth, compost, soil, seeds, pots, trays, building materials for the gardens, a used pickup truck, and advertising.

from one wholesale house to another. And wholesalers, just like retail vendors, also have sales and closeouts.

For a sampling of prices for some of the more common herb craft supplies, take a look at the following:

Tip...

Smart Tip

Package shampoos and other bath products in plastic bottles rather than glass. If the product slides through slippery hands, there's no broken glass to worry about.

- *Essential oils.* Prices vary tremendously with the type of oil you buy. An 8-ounce bottle contains about 200 drops of oil, or enough to scent up to 80 bars of soap or 5 to 20 flacons of toilet water or perfume, depending on recipes. Lavender oil in an 8-ounce size can run anywhere from $18 to $40, while the same size bottle of German chamomile can run upwards of $265.
- *Soap base.* Glycerin soap base, used to make melt-and-pour soaps, goes for $35 to $75 when purchased in 24-pound or 40-pound chunks.
- *Bottles.* Clear plastic bottles with dispensing caps range from $13 for two dozen 4-ouncers to $19 for two dozen 16-ouncers.
- *Wreaths.* Try on a 12-inch wire frame for $1.65, 36 bricks of Oasis for $32, and 1,400 florist's wires for $24.50

All Together Now

Take a look at the business expenses provided by our hypothetical herb farms on page 103. Sage Advice, as you'll recall, will sell potted plants by mail order, at farmers' markets, and to tourists from a rural acre, while Herban Planet will sell fresh-cut herbs to restaurants and specialty stores, as well as herb crafts from plants grown on an urban half acre. Sage Advice has built a 10-foot-by-20-foot greenhouse, using steel pipe hoop framing and 3-millimeter plastic. Herban Planet has purchased two 10-foot-by-20-foot prefab steel-frame, poly-covered greenhouses. With twice as much greenhouse space, Herban Planet has purchased twice as much irrigation system as Sage Advice. Herban Planet has also opted to start off with more seedlings than seeds. Both companies will use vehicles already in the owners' possession.

Tip...

Smart Tip

If you'll sell fresh-cut herbs by weight, you'll need to invest in a legal-for-trade scale. Expect to pay in the range of $400 for an easy-read digital display model. (Some are even battery-powered so you can tote them along to the farmers' market!)

Use the worksheet on page 104 to list your own costs. And don't forget to add your farm start-up costs to your company setup costs (determined in Chapter 7) to get the true picture of how much you'll need to get up and running!

Farm Setup Costs for Hypothetical Business

Costs	Sage Advice	Herban Planet
Growing medium and soil amendments	$600	$1,200
Garden tools	156	956
Greenhouses and accessories	1,886	4,972
Irrigation system	500	1,000
Pots and propagation trays	100	250
Seeds and seedlings	100	250
Potted plant labels	137	0
Farm vehicle	0	0
Weight scale	0	400
Fresh herb packaging supplies	0	0
Compost bin	0	125
Tool shed	500	500
Total Setup Costs	**$3,979**	**$9,653**

Your Farming Start-Up Expenses

Growing medium and soil amendments $ _____

Garden tools   _____

Greenhouse and accessories   _____

Irrigation system   _____

Pots and propagation trays   _____

Seeds and seedlings   _____

Farm vehicle   _____

Weight scale   _____

Compost bin   _____

Tool shed   _____

Fresh herb packaging supplies   _____

Your Total Farming Start-Up Expenses: $ _____

Propagating Profits
Determining Your Bottom Line

Now that you've put together a picture of how much money you'll spend getting your herb business up and running, it's time to figure out how much you can expect to earn—which means you'll first have to determine how much to charge for your products.

▲

And that's what we'll explore in this chapter: pricing your herbs and herbal products and figuring out how much you'll sell. We'll also investigate your annual operating expenses—those ongoing costs like phone service, utilities, and gas for your delivery vehicle—and put it all together to discover how much you'll actually make as an herb farmer.

Pricing Pointers

Your prices will vary, of course, depending on what products you're selling—fresh-cut herbs, starter plants in pots, dried herbs for wreaths, or something else entirely—and they'll also vary based on the going market prices in your area. (This is one reason doing your market research is so important.) Following are three different samples of how to price your products based on whether you'll be selling freshly harvested herbs to local restaurants and markets, selling container herbs locally and by mail order, or selling herb crafts you make yourself.

By the Bunch

You know from your research that one bunch of sweet basil sells at the market for $1.95. This means the market has probably marked up that basil about 60 percent and paid $1.20 for it—which also means that you can't sell it to markets for any more than $1.20 unless you can convince the manager to raise his price.

So let's say you'll mark each bunch of sweet basil at $1.20. From your research, you project Joe's Gourmet Market can sell 20 bunches of your herbs each week. So that's $24 a week income—just for sweet basil. You'll also supply other herbs, of course, for which you'll make the same calculations.

You can project your restaurant sales the same way. Instead of reverse engineering your price based on what a store charges its customers less 50 percent to 60 percent, in the case of restaurants, start with prices your research has shown that chefs are paying (or will pay) for fresh herbs.

> ## Tip...
>
> ### Smart Tip
> Packaging sells. A bar of herbal soap dressed up in tissue and ribbon or tied up in tulle will sell for more money than a plain-Jane bar set out on a shelf.

By the Pot

How do you determine how much to charge for potted plants? You use basically the same method as above: look at how much your competition—garden centers, other mail order herb farmers, or Wal-Mart—charges for the same varieties. Then mark yours at similar rates. If you've got something that sets your potted herbs apart, such as organic growing conditions, fancy decorated containers, or exotic varieties that can't be readily found elsewhere, you may be able to bump up your prices considerably. But again, you'll have to conduct market research to find out.

Take a look at the sample worksheets for figuring profits included in this chapter—you'll see gross annual incomes based on a six-month outdoor growing season and a six-month greenhouse growing season.

We've also provided gross income worksheets (see page 109 and 111) on which you can figure your own earnings. Modify the sheets to fit your own herb business—if you'll have a year-round growing season, for instance, or if you'll sell dried herbs and flowers or herbal bath products, adjust the worksheet accordingly.

Selling Herb Crafts

Pricing herbal crafts requires the same basic technique of competitive pricing—but with an added twist. Unless you make your herbal products entirely from your own plant materials put together with supplies that are scrounged, scavenged, or salvaged, you'll need to consider how much it costs you to make each item before you can decide its price.

If you'll craft wreaths, for instance, you'll need to consider the costs of the Styrofoam or wire base for each one, plus glue, florist's wire, ribbon, spaghnum moss, and any botanicals you don't grow. If you'll manufacture fragrances, you'll need to purchase essential oils, alcohol, and the flasks or vials to bottle them in.

The main idea here, of course, is to use the herbs you grow, and herbal products can be a wonderful way to use plant materials that don't sell as fresh-cut or potted. Take advantage of autumn's end by drying botanicals to use in potpourris, sachets, and other crafts. Then add to your annual income by selling these gems. Take a look at the sample herb craft pricing worksheet on page 112, then work up your own for each product you'll make using the form on pages 113 and 114.

Once you've priced your herb crafts, you've still got yet another step in estimating your annual income: determining how many of each product you'll sell per year. This is basically the same as figuring how many fresh-cut or potted herbs you'll sell, then adding it up.

As you look over the sample worksheet, which covers making bars of soap, you'll note that we've bought the products in bulk from a wholesaler. You'll typically find much better prices with wholesalers than you will if you shop at a retail store, and you can get even better pricing when you purchase your raw materials in bulk. A two-pound bar of soap base, for instance, purchased from a whole-

Beware!

Underpricing your products can be almost as fatal to sales as overpricing. When your wares are priced too low, customers tend to think there's something wrong with them and won't buy.

Figuring Profits on Fresh-Cut Herbs, Part 1

1. List the herbs you can sell each week to restaurants and specialty markets in the spring and summer, your price per bunch, and your total per type of herb:

Herb	No. of Bunches or Packets/Week	Price Per Unit	Total
Sweet basil	100	$1.20	$120.00
Rosemary	100	1.20	120.00
Dill	75	1.20	90.00
Cilantro	100	1.25	125.00
Mint	100	1.20	120.00
Chocolate mint	50	1.25	62.50
Sage	50	1.25	67.50
Lavender	100	1.35	135.00
Thyme	100	1.25	125.00
Nasturtium	50	1.35	67.50
Rose petals	50	1.35	67.50
Weekly total:			**$1,100.00**

2. Multiply the weekly total by the number of weeks in a spring/summer season:
$1,100 x 26 weeks = $28,600

3. List the herbs you can sell each week to restaurants and specialty markets in the fall and winter, your price per bunch, and your total per type of herb:

Herb	No. of Bunches or Packets/Week	Price Per Unit	Total
Sweet basil	20	$1.20	$24.00
Rosemary	20	1.20	24.00
Oregano	20	1.20	24.00
Sage	20	1.25	25.00
Mint	20	1.20	24.00
Chocolate mint	10	1.25	12.50
Arugula	20	1.25	25.00
Fennel	20	1.25	25.00
Thyme	20	1.25	25.00
Chrysanthemum blossoms	20	1.35	27.00
Pansy	20	1.35	27.00
Weekly total:			**$262.50**

4. Multiply the weekly total by the number of weeks in your fall/winter season:
$262.50 x 26 weeks = $6,825.00

5. Add your spring/summer and fall/winter totals to arrive at your gross income:
$28,600 + $6,825 = $35,425

Figuring Profits on Fresh-Cut Herbs, Part 2

1. List the herbs you can sell each week to restaurants and specialty markets in the spring and summer, your price per bunch, and your total per type of herb:

Herb	No. of Bunches or Packets/Week	Price Per Unit	Total

Total $ _____

2. Multiply your weekly total by the number of weeks in your spring/summer growing season:

$_____ x _____ weeks = $ _____

3. List the herbs you can sell each week to restaurants and specialty markets, your price per bunch, and your total per type of herb:

Herb	No. of Bunches or Packets/Week	Price Per Unit	Total

Total $ _____

4. Multiply the weekly total by the number of weeks in your fall/winter growing season:

$_____ x _____ weeks = $ _____

5. Add your spring/summer and fall/winter totals to arrive at your gross annual income:

$_____ + $ _____ = $ _____

▲

Figuring Profits on Potted Herbs, Part 1

1. List the herbs you can sell in the spring and summer and the price per pot (assuming you'll sell only 3-inch pots):

Herb	Price Per Pot
Anise hyssop	$3.50
Bee balm	3.00
Chocolate mint	3.50
Chamomile	3.00
Clary sage	3.50
Lady's bedstraw	3.50
Lavender	3.50
Lemon balm	3.50
Oregano	3.00
Peppermint	3.00
Rose geranium	3.00
Rosemary	3.00
St. John's wort	3.50
Thyme	3.00

2. Multiply your average potted herb price of $3.25 by the number of plants you plan to sell each week during your spring/summer season:

   210 per week x $3.25 = $682.50

3. Multiply this figure by the number of weeks in your spring/summer growing season:

   $682.50 x 26 weeks = $17,745

4. Now list the herbs you'll grow and sell in your greenhouse during your fall/winter season:

Arugula	$3.50
Chocolate mint	3.50
Peppermint	3.00
Rosemary	3.50
Sage	3.00
Thyme	3.00

5. Multiply your average potted herb price of $3.25 by the number of plants you plan to sell each week:

   105 per week x $3.25 = $341.25

6. Multiply this figure by the number of weeks in your fall/winter growing season:

   $341.25 x 26 weeks = $8,872.50

7. Add your spring/summer and fall/winter totals to arrive at your gross annual income:

   $17,745.00 + $8,872.50 = $26,617.50

Figuring Profits on Potted Herbs, Part 2

1. List the herbs you can sell and the price per pot in the spring and summer:

Herb	Price Per Pot

2. Multiply your average potted herb price of $_____ by the number of plants you plan to sell each week during your spring/summer season:

_____ pots per week x $_____ = $_____

3. Multiply this figure by the number of weeks in your spring/summer growing season:

$_____ x _____ weeks = $_____

4. Now list the herbs you'll grow and sell in your greenhouse during your fall/winter season:

5. Multiply your average potted herb price of $_____ by the number of plants you plan to sell each week:

_____ pots per week x $_____ = $_____

6. Multiply this figure by the number of weeks in your fall/winter growing season:

$_____ x _____ weeks = $_____

7. Add your spring/summer and fall/winter totals to arrive at your gross annual income:

$_____ + $_____ = $_____

▲

Figuring Profits on Handcrafted Herbs, Part 1

1. List the materials you'll use for one recipe, which makes four bars of soap:

   $1/2$ lb. (or 2 cups) grated soap base
   $2/3$ cup distilled water
   1 tsp. dried lavender
   $1/2$ tsp. dried thyme
   10 drops lavender essential oil
   5 drops thyme essential oil

2. List your costs per recipe, based on buying your materials in bulk, then add them up:

   Soap base: $0.73 for $1/2$ lb.
   Distilled water: $.08 for $1/3$ cup
   Dried lavender and thyme come from your garden; no direct cost involved
   Lavender oil: $0.90 for 10 drops
   Thyme oil: $0.60 for 5 drops
   Total: $2.31 per recipe

3. Divide your cost per recipe by the number of bars, which is four:

   $$\$2.31 / 4 = \$0.58 \text{ per bar}$$

4. Now decide on your markup (professional crafters often mark up their wares by four times their cost):

   $$\$0.58 \times 4 = \$2.32 \text{ per bar}$$

5. Determine whether you've got a valid price. $2.32 only reimburses you for your raw materials and not for your time, effort, and creativity. And since $2.32 is very low for a handcrafted product (and not any more than you'd pay for scented soap at the grocery store), you might bump up your price by doubling it to $4.64 or even more, depending on what your research shows your market will bear.

6. One more decision: $4.64 is an awkward number. Consumers typically feel more comfortable with a price that ends in .95 or .99. So lower your price to $3.99 or bump it up again to $4.95.

Figuring Profits on Handcrafted Herbs, Part 2

1. List the materials you'll use for one product or recipe (soap bars, wreath, potpourri, etc.):

   _____

   _____

   _____

   _____

   _____

   _____

2. List your costs per product or recipe, based on buying your materials in bulk, and add them up:

   _____

   _____

   _____

   _____

   _____

   _____

   _____

3. Divide your cost per recipe by the number of products it makes (bars, bottles, etc.) if applicable: _____

4. Decide on your markup: _____

5. Determine whether your price is valid, and adjust accordingly: _____

6. Bump your price up or down if necessary to compensate for awkward numbers: _____

▲

Figuring Profits on Handcrafted Herbs, Part 3

On this worksheet, you'll list what crafts you plan to sell and what your sales price will be for each. Keep in mind that this total represents your gross weekly sales. Don't forget to account for your cost of sales, which is the money you pay for materials and supplies. If it costs you $10.51 to make one wreath that you sell for $24.95, you'll have to subtract that off the profit for each product. Remember, too, that some products have higher profit margins than others. Where that bar of soap may cost as little as $0.58 to manufacture, a wreath may cost much more.

Product	No. of Products/ Week	Price	Total
Thymely lavender soap bar	15	$4.95	$74.25
Thymely rosemary body wash	7	7.95	55.65
Thymely lemon/lavender shampoo	7	6.99	48.93
Lemon rosemary massage oil	3	6.99	20.97
Lavender rose geranium potpourri	10	7.95	79.50
Lemon rosemary potpourri	10	7.95	79.50
Cinnamon sage potpourri	10	7.95	79.50
Thymely kitchen culinary wreath	4	24.95	99.80
Eternal summer botanical wreath	5	24.95	124.75
Nature's bounty wreath	4	22.95	91.80
		Total	$754.65

sale soap supplier goes for $5 or $2.50 per pound. Comparatively, a 24-pound shipment costs only $1.46 per pound. You'll save on shipping or travel time as well when you buy in larger quantities.

Cost City

OK, now you know how much you can expect to earn. But you're not done with arithmetic yet. You'll have ongoing operating expenses—the things you pay for every month or every year—to offset all those greenbacks. And until you deduct those costs from your income, you won't really know what your bottom line will be.

Stat Fact

Yes, upscale eateries are worth those delivery trips: Total sales for full-service restaurants soared from just over $39 million to more than $117 million in the most recent 19-year period surveyed, according to the National Restaurant Association.

Supply Side

If you'll sell potted herbs, you'll need pots not just for starting your first herbs but for ongoing sales as well. The number of plants you plan to sell each month—which you've conveniently worked up on your figuring profits worksheet (see page 111)—will tell you how many pots you'll need to buy each month. Don't forget to add in any soil and amendments you may need as well.

If you'll purchase plants to fill in during the growing season or to start new each spring, then you'll need to also count seeds, plugs, and other transplants as operating expenses. Take another look at costs for these items in Chapter 8, then figure out how much you'll need to replenish your stock throughout the year.

Restaurants, markets, and other customers will send your plastic bags or boxes straight to the nearest waste container once they've used the herbs within, so you'll need to replenish these supplies as well. The more you can buy and store at a time, the better prices you'll get. And don't forget labels or hang tags for all your products. Prices for these will vary, of course, depending on what you buy, how much, and from whom. Take another look at our previous chapter for ballpark prices.

As far as other miscellaneous office supplies go, once you've dressed your office with stationery and desk accessories, your ongoing costs should be fairly low—there's a limit to how many staplers, paper clips, and calendars you'll need. Refer to the office supplies shopping chart in Chapter 7 for prices.

Party Time

Celebrate your new herb business with a festive grand opening. Invite friends, family, suppliers, folks on your mailing list, and local news media. Make it an herbal tea party, a tour of your display gardens, or an evening-in-the-garden open house.

Have each partygoer sign a guest book that includes space for her address, which will give you names for your mailing list. Hand out brochures or price lists and perhaps a small nosegay of fresh herbs or sachet of dried scents.

It's a Gas

Your delivery vehicle comes equipped with several ongoing expenses, in addition to any payments you'll make on its purchase price, including gas, maintenance, and insurance. Figure gas by calculating your delivery route mileage, dividing it by your jalopy's miles per gallon and then averaging in gas prices in your area.

Stat Fact

In a recent survey by the U.S. Department of Agriculture, more than 6,000 farmers surveyed at 772 markets said they sell exclusively at farmers' markets.

Let's say, for instance, that you'll deliver to five restaurants each week, racking up a total of 140 miles per week. Your trusty van gets 14 mpg, so you're using 10 gallons of gas each week. Based on gasoline prices in your area of $1.65 per gallon, you can figure on $16.50 per week, or about $65 per month.

Maintenance can include routine oil and lube jobs, as well as trips to the car wash to keep your jalopy looking fresh. You may also want to pencil in a line item to anticipate those inevitable flat tires and worn-out brakes.

Getting the Word Out

Farmers' markets can be terrific venues in which to add to your earnings, increase your visibility to potential customers, and just plain have fun. Fees for farmers' market participation vary widely depending on the region of the country and the popularity of the market—anywhere from $45 to $170 for an entire growing season payable in one lump sum of $5 to $35 per day paid on a first-come, first-served basis.

As we explored in Chapter 7, if you've got a business, you must have separate phone lines. Start with a base rate of $25 per line—one for your business, which is separate

Just in Case

Workers' compensation insurance is an expense you may not have thought of. It covers you for any illness or injury your employees might incur on the job, from a back injury lifting bags of mushroom compost to a case of heat stroke from working in the hot sun.

Even if employees are on the job in your backyard herb farm, which is technically your home, your homeowners insurance won't cover them—you must have separate coverage. Workers' compensation insurance laws vary from state to state; check with your insurance agent for details in your area.

from your home phone, and one for your fax machine and e-mail. Then add in estimated long-distance charges based on where your clients and customers will be located, how often you expect to call them, and what sort of rate you've negotiated with your long-distance carrier.

As your herb business grows, your postage expenses will grow as well. For starters, figuring on an average of two pieces of snail mail per day at the good old first-class rate of 37 cents per piece, you can pencil in about $22 per month. Keep in mind, however, that what we're talking about here is the postage you'll stick on bills and invoices. If you decide to advertise via direct mail or mail order, your postage costs will be much higher.

For routine communications, you'll use e-mail as much or more than you use the U.S. Postal Service. And to use e-mail, you'll need an Internet service provider, or ISP. ISPs generally charge a flat rate of $20 to $25 for unlimited monthly service, which gives you not only e-mail capability but access to the wonderful world of the Web.

If your business will have a Web site, you'll need a Web host, which is the computer or computers that handle all your customer traffic. While you can manipulate your Web site all you want from your personal computer, it takes a much, much larger server to handle the complexities and size of Web traffic, and that's why you need a host. How much can you expect to pay for Web hosting? Plan on a range of $10 to $75 per month.

Operating in the Green

Once you've figured your operating expenses, you can deduct them from your annual profits to put together an income and expense statement and find out how green (or how much in the red) your herb business will be. Take a look at the income and expense statements in Chapter 13 of our hypothetical herb farms, Sage Advice and Herban Planet, then pencil in your own using the worksheet that's also in that chapter.

You'll want to tailor your income statement to your particular business—you may or may not need to ink in figures for items like rent, employee payroll, and workers' compensation insurance. Don't forget to pro-rate items that are paid annually, such as business licenses and tax-time accounting fees, and pop those figures into your yearly statement. If you pay annual insurance premiums of $600, for instance, divide this figure by 12 and add the resulting $50 to your insurance expense.

Smart Tip *Tip...*

If you borrow money to start your business, you'll need to repay the loan, so don't forget to ink in this expense along with your other monthly fees.

The Fund Zone

Now that you've done the math, you may be ready to roll—or not, depending on the state of your wallet. If you can easily afford the start-up funds, go for it. If, on the other hand, your coffers won't stand the strain, you'll have to find financing. But don't worry: You've got those start-up expenses and that projected income statement to show prospective lenders.

You might want to consider financing through your local bank or credit union. Put together a package that includes not only your start-up and income and expense statements but also all the statistics you've gathered in your market research phase on the sunny future of the herb industry.

Most entrepreneurs, however, get a little help from their friends, when they start their new businesses—they borrow from family or friends. This source has several advantages: minimal paperwork, no application fees or lengthy waiting period, and the satisfaction of sharing your business success with your "lender."

But whether you borrow from Great-Aunt Myrtle or your best friend, Bob, keep in mind that it's still a business loan. Figure the repayment of borrowed funds into your costs and treat your repayment agreement as seriously as you would any bank loan.

Many start-up entrepreneurs take a different tack when looking for funds to grow on—their own credit cards. Before you choose this option, take a look at your available credit balances and the annual percentage rates. Card companies frequently offer low rates as an incentive to sign up or to use their service. Go with the one that offers the best rate for the longest period.

> ## Dollar Stretcher
> Consider having a well dug. In some parts of the country, this is relatively inexpensive and can save valuable city water dollars.

> ## Smart Tip
> *Tip...*
> For the best possible impression on your banker, assemble your start-up materials in a professional-looking folder along with your desktop-published brochure or price lists. The more businesslike your company looks, the better.

> ## Smart Tip
> *Tip...*
> Decide on a minimum dollar amount per order and require that chefs order at least that amount of cut herbs each delivery, advises Maureen Rogers of the Herb Growing and Marketing Network. Also, require payment on delivery, as restaurants are notoriously slow payers.

Minding
Your Garden
Operations

You've done your market research, set up your business structure, and got all your finances squared away. Now you can get down to the real fun of working your herb business—sowing, growing, and harvesting your plants as well as preparing them for sale.

In this chapter we'll explore these operations in brief. Techniques vary with the type of herb, as well as the philosophy and temperament of the grower—as a successful herb farmer, it's your responsibility to learn everything you can about nurturing the herbs you plan to sell. Our goal here is to give you the flavor of what your tasks—and your life—as an herb grower will be like.

For intimate details on your herbs of choice, read everything you can. Join herb and gardening associations. Talk to other growers. Call your county extension service. Experiment. And don't be afraid to ask questions—you can't learn if you don't ask!

Charting a Course

One of your biggest tasks as an herb farmer will be designing and charting your garden's growth calendar. Some plants burst into bloom for a single vibrant growing season and then die out. Others shine for two seasons and then fade into compost fodder. And still others take up to five years to mature into herbal production.

You'll have to take each herb's life span into consideration along with how much of each plant you'll need through the year. You can't very well sell brimming baskets of lavender your first year in operation if your plants won't mature for three years or more. And while sweet basil, for instance, is ready to harvest the very first season it's planted, you may want to sow it in weekly or monthly groupings so you don't use up your entire supply in one shot.

Life Cycles

All plants can be characterized as *annuals*, *biennials*, or *perennials*, terms that refer to their natural life spans. Annuals have the shortest lives, maturing, flowering, and dying in a single growing season. Biennials are late bloomers, producing leaves the first growing season, flowering the second, and then dying. Perennials generally get off to the slowest start but also last the longest, dying to the ground in winter but popping back up good as new the next spring for years.

Beware!
Mint has a well-deserved reputation as a rambunctious rambler. Plant it in containers or severely curbed beds, or else be prepared for it to overtake every other plant in the garden.

Annuals are the herb farm's laid-back types, easy to germinate from seed and easy to grow. Many bloom all season long before conveniently producing scads of seeds for next year's growth. Because their root systems are shallow and remain near the soil surface, annuals are usually heavy drinkers requiring lots of water. They're also usually sun lovers who won't be happy in shadow or shade. Lots of annuals can be sown directly in the ground, but some like to be coddled in indoor starter trays until the weather warms up.

Biennials are the adolescents of the herb farm, taking two years from germination to bloom to the end of their life cycle. They start out with lots of lovely foliage in the first season, along with sturdy roots in which to store nutrients for the winter. The second spring, they bloom, then produce seeds, and die.

Because the roots are so important for second-year growth, you should sow biennial seeds directly in the ground or in peat pots that can be planted in the ground come spring. This way you avoid accidentally damaging the root system.

Perennials are the herb farm's old-timers, plants that take up to five years to mature but grow for years. As TV gardener Rebecca Kohls exhorts, "The first year they sleep, the second year they creep, and the third year they leap."

Some perennials, like lavender, need to be divided after they reach full maturity to prevent them from getting crotchety and nonproductive. But others, like mint, will not only continue to produce but will spread unchecked unless you step in and thin them out. Certain perennials can be germinated from seed, while others, like French tarragon, don't even produce seeds. The best way to propagate most perennials is with cuttings or by division.

Now, that's the basic textbook version of herb life cycles. In practice, it's not quite so cut and dried. Some herbs, like marjoram, are classified as perennials because of the way they grow in their native warm and drowsy Mediterranean climate. But Northern-zone gardeners must treat them as annuals because they die in winter and have to be resown each spring. Other herbs, like biennial parsley, have to be replanted each year because they're grown for their leaves and not for their second-season flowers.

Making Your Beds

You can't take just any old dirt, stick in a plant and expect it to thrive. Soil that's never been used for gardening is most likely too full of sand, clay, rocks, debris, or weeds, or is just plain nutrient-deficient. Even good garden loam that's been carefully tended all season will need a nutrient boost the next spring to replace minerals consumed by the previous year's crops.

As an herb entrepreneur, you'll devote a good part of each spring to prepping new fields and pepping up your presently used ones. This is where you get all that good,

Smart Tip

Carefully follow seed packet directions for depth, date, and soil temperature when planting seeds outdoors. Don't forget to keep them moist, but don't drown them in heavy hose spray, either.

free aerobic exercise—wielding shovels, tillers, rakes, and hoes; toting rocks, bricks, or timbers to build up planting beds; and lugging bags of soil amendments and fertilizers. It's hard work that results in a lot of blisters but also in a glow of accomplishment that can't be matched by a job as a desk jockey.

You'll also spend time in the fall bedding down your plants for the winter. You'll clear the last of summer's weeds and leaf debris, trim back any dead or dying top growth, and tuck your outdoor plants into snug and cozy blankets of mulch. You'll also bring any plants you want to grow indoors into the greenhouse.

During winter, you'll tend greenhouse plants, pore over your garden plans and journals to see what went right or wrong and why, and make lots of wish lists from mail order seed catalogs. Then, as the worst of winter fades, you'll pull back mulch, prune dead branches, clear more leaf debris, and get everything spruced up for spring's arrival.

New Arrivals

Spring is traditionally planting time, but if you'll have a greenhouse or other indoor germination space, you can fiddle with the calendar a bit. Choose a date that represents the finale of frost in your region and then work back six to eight weeks on the calendar. This is the time to sow seeds indoors.

Use any growing container you like, but the best options are flats, or peat pots, nifty little minipots of planting medium cradled in a sort of cheesecloth that dissolves when placed in the ground. If you use flats or other containers, you'll later remove tender seedlings from the planting medium and plant them in the ground. With peat pots, you just stick the whole thing—loam and seedling together—into outdoor beds so you don't risk damaging baby root systems.

Place newly sown herbs in your greenhouse, in a sunny window or under grow lights. Seedlings are sun-worshippers, preferring 10 to 15 hours of light a day. Keep

Extra! Extra!

It's always smart to plant more than you think you'll sell. By doing so, you solve several possible dilemmas at once. You have extra plants you can afford to "feed" to garden critters or bugs and extra stock on hand if sales are better than you projected.

You can always pot extra seedlings instead of bedding them in the ground. Then use them for fresh-cut or dried product or sell them as potted plants to nurseries, health-food stores, farmers' markets, or swap meets, or even set up a booth at a local college campus.

them moist, but not wet. And keep them cozy. Most preemie herbs will germinate at temperatures of 65 degrees to 75 degrees Fahrenheit. If your greenhouse or indoor space isn't warm enough, you can keep those seeds cuddly with electric heating mats.

As the soil warms in your fields or garden, you'll harden off your seedlings to get them used to outdoor life. Like sending your children to preschool in short forays to acclimatize them to the outside world, you place seedlings outdoors for one or two hours a day, working them up to a full-time life in the elements before transplanting them into beds.

Care and Feeding

Herbs have a reputation in the plant world for being carefree folks you can plant and then ignore. While they're certainly more easygoing than, say, picky hothouse types like orchids and violets, you can't just love 'em and leave 'em. You'll need to spend a considerable amount of time in weeding, pest control, and fertilizing tasks.

Weeding Out Trouble

Weeds like well-tended, fertile garden loam as much as your coveted herbs do—and weeds aren't shy about invading somebody else's territory. So one of your biggest tasks will be weed control. Since one of your selling points is organic, chemical-free crops, you can't (and won't want to) use chemical herbicides. Try these all-natural methods instead:

- *Plow up any and all weeds in late fall to prevent surprise reappearances come spring.* Don't toss "harvested" weeds into the compost pile, or you'll end up with weed seeds ticking away like tiny time bombs in your newly-created loam.

- *Tuck herbs in with mulch, even in summer.* Mulch smothers weeds, blocking sunlight so they can't thrive, and also helps keep moisture in the soil so herb roots don't dry out as quickly. You can recycle lots of organic materials to make your own mulch: fresh-mown grass (so long as it's weed-free), chopped straw or seaweed, cocoa hulls, pine straw, or bark.

- *Get in there and weed regularly.* It's therapeutic (for you, not the weeds), easy if you don't wait until weeds are full-fledged monsters, and can be a good way for junior farmers to earn spending money.

Unwelcome Visitors

Bugs may be among the least welcome of earth's life forms, but they don't let a cold shoulder from farmers stand in the way of a good meal. They'll cheerfully invite themselves to a full-course dinner on your fresh herbs and stay all summer. It's up to you to fend them off—and, again, as an organic gardener, you can't rush out and buy the arsenal of chemical insecticides you'll find on the market. There are, however, organic ways to fight back, including the following:

- *Let your fingers do the stalking.* Pick insects off your plants by hand and then give them the heave-ho in a bucket of soapy water.
- *Suck them into oblivion with the wand of your trusty vacuum cleaner.* Be sure to dispose of the vacuum bag afterward so they can't crawl out and back into your world.
- *Give 'em the Mr. Clean routine by washing them away with a blast from the garden hose.* Take care not to knock over or bruise tender plants—this method is for sturdier plants that can take the treatment.
- *Cover plants with a lightweight garden cloth that lets the sun shine in but keeps bugs out*—but don't use where temperatures exceed 75 degrees Fahrenheit, or plants can overheat.
- *Trim away badly infested leaves or branches* and dispose of them where insects can't return to haunt healthy plants.
- *Mix up your own organic insecticides* using ingredients like cayenne pepper, Tabasco sauce, and minced garlic whirled in the blender, then apply with a sprayer. Wash plants thoroughly after harvest—you don't want your chocolate mint to taste like garlic!
- *Drown 'em in drink.* Place saucers or jar lids filled with beer in slug and snail-infested areas. They'll go for the gusto, slither right in, and drown themselves. Take care not to use this method where pets or children could drink the beer.
- *Fight bugs with bugs.* Purchase ladybugs, green lacewings, and encarsia formosa, a tiny wasplike creature. These good-guy insects eat aphids and whiteflies and won't harm your herbs. The only drawback here is that unless you place them in a closed

The Fertile Edge

Stroll the aisles of any garden center, and you'll see rows of fertilizers of all types, strengths, and materials. Fertilizers come in synthetic and organic varieties. You can choose from water-soluble brands that you can apply as you water, powdered or granulated fertilizers that you sprinkle on or mix into the soil, and resin-coated brands that you mix in or sprinkle atop loam.

If you're an organic farmer, you'll want to go with fertilizers derived from organic materials, including fish emulsion, bone meal, seaweed, composted manure, and even bat guano. The best part about going organic with fertilizers is that they build up not only your herbs but your soil as well for an all-round healthy farm environment.

environment like a greenhouse, they may fly off to buggier pastures.

- *Practice companion planting.* Herbs like thyme and pennyroyal repel some insects, while other herbs, like fennel, attract good gals like ladybugs.

Smart Tip *Tip...*

Small lizards make good guardians of the greenhouse, eating bad-guy bugs but not plants.

Reaping the Harvest

Once you've nurtured your herbs to maturity, it's time to harvest. Traditionally, this means waiting until fall to mow down great fields of wheat or corn beneath an amber harvest moon. For the herb farmer, harvest season can be anytime during the growing season that plants are ready to be cut, plucked, trimmed, or pulled up.

The best time of day to harvest herbs is in the early morning, after the dew has evaporated but before the sun begins to heat plants' essential oils and burn off their characteristic aromatic qualities. (If you must pick at a later hour, go ahead. You won't ruin your herbs, but do try for a morning harvest.)

If you pick wet herbs, you'll have to dry them before you can store or package them or they'll quickly rot, so don't water right before harvesting. You may want to give them a good shower the day before picking to wash away dust, mud or dirt. Or wait until after cutting to gently swish dirty (or buggy) herbs in a cool water bath, then blot with paper towels to dry or whisk them around in a salad spinner.

Before you get to the paper towel/salad spinner stage, you'll have to actually reap those herbs. All you need is a pair of sharp scissors or a garden knife, a container in which to stash cut herbs, rubber bands, and—if the weather is hot—a cooler packed with towel-covered ice or freezer gel-packs to keep your herbs cool and fresh while you work.

You can either cut several leaves and stems at a time or cut them individually, depending on whether they're all about the same height, like chives, or whether they're different lengths, like oregano. Check each cutting for blemishes, dirt, and bugs as you go—if you see something you can't easily remedy in the field or processing area (like badly aphid-infested leaves; brown, dry tips; or evidence of late-night caterpillar snacking), leave it for now or prune it away and go on to the next plant. You want all your herbs to look their best for your buyers. While you harvest herbs, you'll also harvest delighted grins from yourself—reaping the bounty of your labors is a rush!

Smart Tip *Tip...*

If you'll sell your fresh-cut herbs in bunches or dry them in bunches, you'll find it saves time to wrap them with rubber bands while you're harvesting. Be careful, though, not to bruise tender stems!

A Harvest Sampler

There are different techniques for harvesting different types of herbs—to explore the best methods for each would require an encyclopedic text. You'll learn how best to work with the herbs you'll grow by learning from other growers and through your own experimentation.

To give you a how-to sampler, however, take a look at fresh-cut harvest techniques for the following six popular herbs:

- *Basil.* Cut stems just above the next leaf clusters with clean scissors or by pinching with your (clean!) fingers. Pick leaves at the top of the plant first to encourage bushiness instead of spindly behavior. Nip flower buds to promote new growth—once basil flowers and begins to seed, its growing season is over. Include a few buds or blossoms with stems if you like—they can make a nice presentation. For retail and direct wholesale customers, aim for half an ounce to 2 ounces per package or bunch.

- *Dill.* Clip or pick stems, harvesting older, larger foliage before newer, center leaves to encourage new growth and keep this delicate, ferny plant happy. You'll want half-ounce to 1½ ounce packages or bunches for retail and direct wholesale customers.

- *Mint.* Cut or pick mint stems just above the next leaf clusters. Mint is such a boisterous herb that there's not a lot to worry about in harvesting—it just keeps on growing. Make sure clipped stems have healthy green tips instead of brown or moldy ones. Strive (which isn't hard) for 1-ounce to 2-ounce packages or bunches for your retail and direct wholesale customers.

- *Rosemary.* Snip rosemary stems with clean scissors, keeping the sprigs fairly even in length. For those retail and direct wholesale customers, you can sell 1-ounce packets or bunches of stems, or strip the leaves to sell in bags and then market the bare stems as rosemary skewers for use in grilling foods.

- *Sage.* Pick leaves by clipping with scissors or pinching with your clean fingers. Harvest at leaf junctions to promote bushy instead of spindly behavior. Package aromatic sage in 1-ounce to 1½ ounce packets or bunches for retail and direct wholesale customers.

- *Thyme.* Clip or pick tender stems just above the next leaf clusters. Avoid old, woody stems that aren't edible, but do—if you like—include a few edible thyme flowers for show. For retail and direct wholesale customers, thyme should be packaged in ¼ ounce to 1-ounce bunches or packets.

> ## Tip... Smart Tip
> Since some distributors will package your herbs themselves, ask how they want your greens delivered—in quart or gallon bags, for instance, or in bunches.

Cut and Dried

If you plan to sell dried herbs for use in the kitchen, as crafts items or as potpourri, you'll need to dry them after harvest. Improperly dried herbs will soon turn limp and moldy, so choose an area that's dry, dark, and well-ventilated, and if possible, also select a time when the weather is low in humidity. If you're in a high-humidity area, like south Florida in midsummer, for instance, compensate for Mother Nature with fans, an air conditioner, or even a dehumidifier if necessary.

Place cut herbs on screens or tie them in bunches about 1 inch in diameter, then hang them from clothes hangers, rafters or anyplace accessible yet out of the way. If you don't have a professional drying shed, you can let your attic fill in.

Another option is to set herbs on baking sheets in your oven with the pilot light on or with the temperature set at warm (about 150 degrees Fahrenheit—the ideal drying temperature is 90 to 110 degrees). Since thicker-leafed herbs will dry faster than those with thin or very small leaves, don't mix and match types. Leave herbs in the oven for three to six hours with the door ajar if necessary.

Some experts suggest drying herbs in the microwave as yet another option; others say this compromises quality. If you want to give it a try, place your herbs in the nuker between sheets of paper towels, place a cup of water inside, and dry for a minute—more or less—at a low setting. Watch as carefully as you do microwave popcorn, and stop if you see sparks.

As a final option, you can invest in a dehydrator, which will dry herbs faster than the air method and cost anywhere from $40 to $200.

How do you know when herbs are dry? They should be dry to the touch and crumble easily. Depending on the process you use, your indoor air quality and the weather, this can take one minute, several hours, or two weeks or more.

Keeping Their Cool

Once your herbs are dry, you can sell them as stems or bunches, strip leaves and flowers to use in teas and potpourris, or crush them for culinary use. While you've seen all those magazine photos of dried herbs hanging in decorative bunches from

Smart Tip

Use nylon instead of metal screens for drying or lay a length of cotton cloth over metal to prevent metallic changes to your herbs.

Bright Idea

Get creative with dried herbs and flowers. Entrepreneur Ralph C. in Elizabethtown, Pennsylvania, grows a large selection that varies with the season. Besides the usual Sweet Annie and lavenders, among his choices are four different oreganos, several chives, feverfew, yarrow, tansy, lamb's ears, and a variety of bee balms.

kitchen rafters, this is not a look to emulate unless you're going for a strictly decorative effect.

Instead, you'll want to store all dried herb products in airtight containers away from any bright light. Dried herbs like to be cool, dry, in the dark, and collected—moisture will cause rot or mold and bright light and heat will break down the essential oils that make them fragrant and tasty. Get creative and stash your herbs in tins, jars, or even plastic bags with the air squooshed out. And don't forget to label them—you may not remember in three months which was the thyme and which was the oregano.

Package Deal

In our consumer-oriented society, packaging is a big deal. People are attracted as much—or more—by a product's container, label, and display as they are by the product itself. Putting your fresh, organic herbs in a cardboard box emblazoned with cartoon characters or the words "New! Improved!" isn't exactly the way to go. But you can do a lot to give your products eye appeal and convince customers to buy them.

Pretty in Green

For retail and direct wholesale customers of fresh-cut herbs, you've got three main packaging options for gussying up those greens. The one you choose is up to you—and, of course, to what your research tells you your customers will find smart and pretty. Here's the scoop on each:

- *Plastic bags*. They look neat and clean, but tender loose-packed leaves can be easily bruised during packaging and any moisture will easily collect, causing herbs to quickly rot.

Mix It Up

Get inventive! Mix several different fresh herbs to sell as your own "private label" blends. Try for something like these, or design your own:

- ❍ Mix arugula, thyme, sage, and oregano for a Mistral Mediterranean Salad blend.
- ❍ Package up chocolate mint, pineapple mint, and peppermint as a Dessert Cook's Delight.
- ❍ Put together nasturtium, lavender, and rose blossoms with lemon balm for a Simply Spring salad starter mix.

- *Plastic clamshell trays.* You may have seen these sturdy little plastic containers with self-locking lids at the grocery store. They make a nice presentation and are easy to stack and store. But they're more expensive than bags or bunches, and again, if moisture collects, the herbs within will quickly rot.
- *Rubber bands or twist-ties.* This is perhaps the simplest, easiest, and cheapest way to go. Unless your herbs need washing and drying, you can prepare bunches as you harvest. You don't have to buy bags or boxes that will later go to the landfill, so you're also being earth-friendly.

Get creative with dried herb packaging. Tie bunches of lavender, yarrow, or sweet Annie with ribbon, raffia, or utilitarian but trendy twine. Swaddle potpourri in gathered squares of muslin, lace, or tulle and tie with ribbons, or pack in neatly sealed cellophane bags, in odd-shaped boxes or jars, or even in good-sized shells. Bundle dried herbs with grapevine or straw wreaths for do-it-yourself kits. Let your imagination soar!

You can get creative with dried herbs for culinary use as well, packaging them in jars, boxes or paper or cellophane bags. But check with local health authorities first to make sure your materials comply.

Don't forget your potted plant sales! While nurseries and garden centers are perfectly happy with the usual 3-inch and 6-inch plastic pots, they'll also be delighted to take a selection of gift or decorative plants. Try pottery or ceramic containers—or even good old plastic ones—dressed to the nines with ribbons, raffia, beads, or buttons.

Fine Print

Once you've decided on containers—be they bags, boxes, or jars—for your herbs, you'll need to think about labels. Even herbs sold in bunches should have hang tags identifying the products and you as the grower. Purchase ready-made labels and print your information using your computer. You can also go eclectic with handcrafted designs—use rubber stamps to add the particulars of each herb. Keep in mind that fresh-cut herbs can—and probably will—get wet, so your labeling should be waterproof.

Each label or hang tag should contain your company name, address, and phone number, as well as the ingredients and their quantity or weight. As a small grower, you're not required to add a nutritional breakdown, although this may change at some point in time. (If in doubt, check with the FDA.)

It never hurts to add the words "organic" and "grown locally" (providing, of course, that it's true). It's also a nice touch to add your farm logo to your labels and hang tags. Herbs are in fashion, so go with the flow. The more upscale and professional your products appear, the more sales appeal they'll have.

> **Beware!**
> If packaging culinary-use herbs in plastic bags, use only food-grade bags that won't leach chemicals into your products—it's required by law.

Plant People
Dealing with Customers and Employees

Even though much of your time will be spent puttering around in your greenhouse and gardens with no distractions but the birds and the bees, you'll still have to spend some time dealing with customers, employees, and other non-herbaceous life forms. In this chapter, we'll explore servicing accounts, working the farmers' market, interacting with retail customers, and handling employees

Make Someone Happy

Once you've convinced specialty markets, restaurants, crafts outlets, or other direct wholesale customers to carry your herbs, you may think you've got it made. This is true—to a certain extent. But that doesn't mean you can rest on your laurels. You'll still devote a fair amount of time each week to servicing those accounts, keeping them up to date on new ways to use the herbs you're already growing, and eliciting their interest in new herbs you may plan to grow. You'll deal with problems, find out if the quantities they've

Photo© PhotoDisc Inc.

ordered are adequate, and in general keep them happy with your products.

Try to schedule deliveries when owners, chefs, or department managers—the people in charge of buying—are onsite and available. You want them to see your herbs at their absolute peak, just after you've picked, packed, and delivered them. If you can't talk to them at delivery time, call later to check up.

While herbs are indeed chic, most people are familiar only with the old standbys—basil, chives, rosemary, and dill. In some parts of the country, cilantro is still considered exotic, while herbs like epazote and sorrel are downright weird. But that's only because they're unknowns.

If you want to grow these "newcomers," you'll have to be able to sell them. And that means teaching. Instead of merely suggesting a new herb (or even an old favorite), approach your accounts with suggested uses and even recipes printed on convenient cards or fliers. This works for everybody from chefs to market managers and can even work

> **Beware!**
> Never use a copyrighted recipe—one found in a cookbook, magazine, or the back of a box of sugar—without permission.

for buyers of potted plants. You might also consider printing recipes or suggested uses on hang tags. People are much more willing to try something new when they know how to go about it.

To Market, to Market

If you can work a farmers' market (which can also be called a green market) into your schedule, by all means do so. It's a great way to add to your income, but even more, it helps make a name for your farm, yourself, and your products. You can educate consumers on using herbs and on herbal lore—which will have the domino effect of getting herbs better known all around town so that more stores and restaurants will want to buy them from you, too.

Farmers' markets are held in growing season all over the country, sponsored by rural counties, midsize townships and greater metropolitan cities. You may find just one in your back-roads region or several held on the same day in different parts of a large urban area. If you can choose from more than one, do some market research before you pay your fees to find out which ones attract more shoppers and which are on the sad-and-slow side.

Once you've chosen, follow these rules for farmers' market sales success:

- *Come early, and come prepared.* You want to be set up and ready to sell when the market opens, not fumbling to set up your table, chair, umbrella, and products while potential buyers pass you by.

- *Some markets assign selling space on a first-come, first-served basis.* Others designate spaces for the entire season. If yours is the former variety, try to get the same spot each market day or one as close as possible to the same spot. This helps previous customers find you among the other vendors.

- *Wear something that will help identify you to customers*—a farmer's straw hat, a chef's apron imprinted with your farm logo, a granny dress and bonnet if it fits your farm niche (and you're female), or even a retro pair of bib overalls and a red kerchief. People who don't remember your name can ask for "the herb person in the overalls" or "the herb lady with the old-fashioned outfit" and be directed to you.

- *Be friendly!* Make eye contact with people as they approach your stall. Ask

Bright Idea

"We have a free sample every week," says Donna F. of her farmers' market stall in Midland, Michigan. "Each week we promote something—mixes, a tea, a dish with fresh herbs. One week we might do a cheese torta with basil. At the peak of cilantro time, we might do a guacamole and have extra bunches of cilantro on hand."

if they've seen your farm-fresh basil, if they'd like to sample your chocolate mint or pick up a free recipe card, or if there's anything you can help them with. Don't be shy—more than half the fun of the farmers' market is talking with people. But don't be pushy either. If shoppers seem shy or uninterested, let them pass without a harangue. Plenty of other buyers will come along.

Reaching Out

Mail order is a cool way to increase your customer base and your income no matter how out-of-the-way your herb business might be or how small you start out. You can sell herbs, plants, seeds, and every sort of herbal product—even workshops and lectures—by advertising in magazines, newspapers, and on the Internet. (We explore advertising in depth in Chapter 12.)

Perhaps surprisingly, there's also a considerable market for container herbs by mail. While you might think tender plants wouldn't survive the rigors of days in dark boxes at the mercy of the U.S. Postal Service, you'd be wrong. Properly packaged, most herbs do just fine. Some herbal entrepreneurs who sell live plants by mail produce thick, glossy, four-color catalogs; others send out homey and homespun

Alive and Well?

How do you ensure that the plants you sell and ship by mail reach their new homes alive and well? It's all in the packing, says Michele B. in Soddy Daisy, Tennessee, who says the very first thing to know is to learn from your mistakes. Here's her tested and proven method:

"First, water plants several hours before shipping so the soil is moist but not dripping," Michele says. "Second, I wrap a small sandwich-sized plastic bag around the bottom of the pot and crisscross two rubber bands over the top and bottom of the pot. This anchors the plant and prevents soil from coming out. Third, I lay the plant on its side and roll it up in newspapers so all you can see is the top of the plant. Fourth, on top of a layer of shipping peanuts, I set each plant against the side of the box and strap it in with packing tape.

"Once all the plants are in their 'seatbelts,' I fill the remaining airspace with peanuts or shredded paper and seal the box tight, weigh it, put a shipping label on it, and out the door to the post office it goes. I send an instruction sheet along explaining how to unwrap the order, give it a drink, set it out in the shade for a day or two, and then plant. Sounds more complicated than it really is!"

▲

Beware!

Be sure to check with the U.S. Department of Agriculture for a list of which states you may not ship plants to, warns mail order herb farmer Michele B. in Soddy Daisy, Tennessee. "The reasons are various," she says, "from fear of infestation of certain insects to not allowing a certain plant into a state because it's classified as a weed—like kudzu, which could take over."

black-and-white minicatalogs, and still others sell only through their Web sites.

Even though you may never come face to face with your mail order customers, you'll want to give them the same personal, one-on-one attention you'll shower on customers with whom you deal directly. This means sending orders quickly, offering tips and advice, and being generous with customer appreciation.

Playing by the Rules

Being good at mail order also means you'll have to play by the rules—not just the ones of common courtesy and customer satisfaction, but also the ones set forth by the FTC.

The FTC's Mail or Telephone Order Rule regulates all businesses involved in direct marketing, which includes orders placed by mail or phone, as well as by fax, e-mail, and the Internet. Despite the fact that the rules were devised by a government entity, they're easy to understand and follow:

- *You must send ordered merchandise within the time period specified in your advertising or, if you don't specify a shipping time, within 30 days.* The clock starts ticking on this time requirement when you receive the completed order. An order is complete when you have received your customer's cash, check, or money order, or charged the person's credit card account, and you have all the information you need to process and ship the order. If the customer doesn't specify essential information, such as size or color preferences, the order is considered incomplete.

- *If you don't specify a shipping time and your customer is applying for credit to pay for the purchase, you have 50 days to ship after receiving the order.* This is the one exception to the 30-day shipping rule.

- *If you can't meet the shipping deadline, you must notify your customer and offer an alternative option.* The customer can either receive a prompt refund or agree to a delay. Your notice must include a new shipping date, instructions on how to cancel the order, and a postage-paid way to reply.

- *If your customer agrees to a new shipping date and you can't meet it again, you must send a second notice as soon as possible.* Unless the customer signs and returns

Smart Tip

Plant yourself in the know about everything mail order with Entrepreneur's business start-up guide, *Start Your Own Mail Order Business.*

this second postage-paid notice, you must automatically cancel the order and refund the person's money.

- *If you can't ship the merchandise on time and you don't notify your customer as required, you must count the order as canceled and send a refund.*

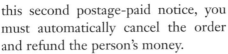

Smart Tip
Get your own complete copy of the Mail or Telephone Order Rule from the FTC at www.ftc.gov.

- *If your customer cancels an order, you must refund his or her money.* If the order was paid for by cash, check, or money order, you must return the money within seven business days. If the order was paid for by credit card, you must credit the customer's credit card account within one billing cycle.

You can legally cheat when you sell plants or seeds, because the rules don't apply to them. But heads up—all other herbal products do apply, except orders shipped c.o.d. (cash on delivery), and magazine subscriptions after the first order.

Team Effort

As your herb business grows and your business expands, you may discover at some point that you need employees—which can be a good thing or a headache. Employees

Growing Relationship

As an herb farmer, your job description covers it all, from planting, harvesting, and picking to packing, shipping, sales, marketing, and product development. But don't ignore the value of spending quality time with your customers.

"During the summer, we have 21 people on our crew," says Mike R., the lavender grower in Sequim, Washington. "Even so, Jadyne and I make a concerted effort to have one or the other of us around—not working or assembling but just schmoozing. Our sales go up exponentially when we're around."

Part of the magic, for customers of Mike and Jadyne at any rate, is having seen the couple and their farm on HGTV's show *"The Good Life."* "We've heard a thousand times about folks seeing us on TV," Mike says. "People tell us, 'After that show, we felt like you were our family.'"

But it's not all lights, action, and cameras. "The farm is our baby," Mike says. "And nobody does it like you—even when we coach our staff. Being accessible really keeps people coming back and staying longer."

can make your job easier and more fun and can promote a sense of family, both within your company and among your customers. But employees also mean increased responsibilities. Instead of being a free-and-easy independent gardener, you become a boss who has to meet payroll, purchase workers' compensation insurance, and cough up quarterly payroll taxes. Then you have to be able to delegate authority, which is easy for some people and as hard as getting rid of chokeweed for others.

An alternative to hiring employees is to turn your family into farm assistants. Kids can pull weeds; plant seedlings; harvest herbs; put together potpourri, wreaths or other herbal products; package mail order products; and assist customers in your shop or greenhouse. Older kids often achieve guru level when it comes to computer tasks—give them your Web site design or data entry duties and let 'em roll.

Don't relegate the work just to kids—a willing spouse or significant other can do just as much, as well as develop (and test) recipes, lay garden paths, or build plant beds and greenhouse benches.

With your own kid-type seedlings in your league as assistants, you don't have to worry about employee taxes or workers' compensation insurance. You'll probably still have payroll, but you can base it on age instead of on market rates. And best of all, providing you don't turn into a tyrant, working in a family business can give kids a great sense of values and self-worth. "One reason I started this business," says Donna F., the farmers' market purveyor in Midland, Michigan, "was to give my kids exposure to a safe environment, teach them a work ethic, and help them fine-tune their math skills making change."

Cool Hand Help

If family labor is not an option or if you reach the point where you need more employees than you have kids and spouses, you'll have to hire help. Try these tips for finding the coolest of farm hands:

- *Interns.* Take on an aspiring high school or college student to design and update your Web site, create marketing materials, write articles and press releases, or work in the greenhouse. Obviously, you'll hire a horticulture student for greenhouse work and a liberal arts major for the marketing stuff, so choose wisely. Interns generally work for a single season for a minimal salary or even for free in exchange for a learning experience and a terrific job to list on their fledgling resumes. To find an intern, place ads on school bulletin boards, go to school placement centers, or talk to instructors and career counselors.

> **Fun Fact**
> Abraham Lincoln founded the Department of Agriculture in 1862, calling it the "people's department." With good reason—at that time, 90 percent of Americans were farmers.

▲

- *Kid power*. Much of farm work is seasonal; seeding, weeding, and harvesting takes place during the spring and summer in most areas of the country. Hire high school and college kids to help out during spring and summer breaks. They'll love the extra income and won't have to go on the dole when the season, and their jobs, are over for the year. Place ads on school bulletin boards, go to school placement centers, or talk to instructors and career counselors for help on finding those cool hands.

- *Magic moms*. Moms of school-age kids make great part-time employees. They like to work while the children are in school so they can go home in the afternoons, which makes them good candidates for those morning harvesting and packing tasks as well as for herb crafting. Ask moms in your neighborhood, your kid's school and activity groups, or your local house of worship.

- *Seniority*. Seniors also make terrific part-time employees. They excel at everything from minding the shop to making and packing products to nursing seedlings. Post ads in seniors centers, community centers, and other senior hot spots.

Herbal Helpers

What positions will you need to hire employees to fill? That depends on your particular business—whether you'll tend a small suburban-sized plot or a large rural

---

Open for Business

Time always seems to be an issue, no matter who you are or what you're doing. As an herb entrepreneur, you won't be locked into the 9-to-5 grind; instead, you'll flow with the rhythm of the seasons—which is one of the perks of going into this business.

But if you plan any sort of retail operation—a shop, tea room, or minigarden center—you'll need to reconsider the time thing and set up some sort of regular hours. You can be open for business every day, for instance, from 9 to 5; only on weekends from 10 to 6; or exclusively on Tuesdays and Thursdays from 10 to 8.

Choose a schedule that works for you and your customers. Keep in mind that you can't stick that "Gone Fishin'" sign in the window whenever you feel like it and amble on down to the swimming hole. One of the quickest ways to lose customers is to be closed when they expect you to be open. So once you've posted your hours, stick to them.

acreage, deliver products to customers, or have them come to your retail shop, sell at fairs or farmers' markets, make herbal crafts, run a restaurant, tea room, or display garden, ship products wholesale, or some combination thereof.

Depending on your needs (at the outset of your business and as you grow), you may consider the following areas for herbal assistance:

- Growing and harvesting

- Packing and shipping

- Crafting

- Retail sales (assisting customers in your shop, at fairs and farmers' markets, or via Internet, mail, and telephone orders)

- Wholesale sales (generating orders from other businesses)

- Delivery drivers

- Advertising and marketing (creating ads, brochures, direct-mail pieces, press releases, labels, your Web site, and other print material)

- Bookkeeping/accounting (handling payroll, record-keeping, bill-paying, and accounts receivable)

Naturally, you'll want your growers to have green thumbs, your salespeople to be great at sales, and your crafting and advertising staff to be talented and creative. But these descriptions are generalizations that don't get down to the nitty-gritty of the tasks you'll want your employees to handle and the necessary qualifications.

Before you put the word out, place an ad, or begin interviewing, draw up a job description. You might decide, for instance, that you want a full-time employee for your small herb garden shop to assist customers, pack your occasional mail orders, make wreaths, and pot, water, and prune container plants. You might seek a part-time bookkeeper who will answer phones in addition to keeping up your accounting. Or you may want a harvester to cut and bind your crops just during the summer season. The clearer and more detailed the job description, the easier it will be to hire the right employee—if you don't know what you want, you can't readily find it.

Spell out the specific tasks you want your new employee to handle, as well as the days and hours you'll need him or her to work. Think, too, about personalities—do you want an independent self-starter capable of functioning without much input from you, or will you be happier with an employee who waits for directions? A perky chatterbox or the strong, silent type?

Decide how much you can afford to pay, then look at ads for similar positions in your local newspaper. Is your rate commensurate with others in your area? If you're too low, you won't likely get any takers (or at least any you'd want). If you can't afford to match local wages, get creative and look for interns or part-timers until you can afford a full-time assistant.

Herbal Attraction

Now write an ad that will attract your ideal employee while discouraging dubious candidates. Try something like this:

Gardener/crafter/salesperson
Wanted for small but busy herb garden/shop. Sales experience a must; gardening and crafting skills a plus. Weekends required. Send resume to:
P.O. Box 1111,
Cottage Garden, GA 55555.

Unless you want to be inundated with phone calls, specify that resumes are to be mailed—this has the added benefit of immediately weeding out prospects who can't make the effort. (If, however, you're hiring harvesters or other low-skill employees who probably won't have resumes, you may choose to put in a phone number.)

Go through the resumes (or applications, which you can buy at office supply stores) and choose the candidates that sound the best; then call them in for interviews.

Ask prospects to describe their work history—not a "what I did on my summer vacation" recitation of their job descriptions, but what they liked best as well as least and why, and what they feel they accomplished in previous jobs. This will give you important clues as to their actual experience as well as their modus operandi—team player, loner, self-starter, or slacker. This is a little scary—after all, you're hiring not just an employee but a helpmate for your brainchild, your baby—your business. But it can also be fun.

Take your time and relax. You may find a ready-to-go candidate with the perfect mix of experience and skills, or you may find one with little or no experience but the perfect personality who'll be a snap to mold and train to your ways. The only mistake you can make is by hiring an employee about whom you have doubts just to fill the space.

Growing Your Business
Advertising and Marketing

Even though herbs are tremendously popular today, they can't sell themselves. And your customers won't likely beat a path to your greenhouse door unless you entice them with summer—and winter—savory advertising and marketing. You don't need a Madison Avenue-sized ad budget or an infomercial starring Ed McMahon running 24 hours a day; all it takes is a lot of enthusiasm, a little chutzpah, and a belief in your herbal products.

In this chapter, we'll explore the elements of herbal advertising, from print ads and press releases to direct mail, workshops, and lectures. You'll learn what it takes to woo, dazzle, and delight potential and present customers—and keep 'em coming back for more.

Have a Plan

Just as you revisit your garden plan each spring before setting out new plants, the first thing to do before starting your advertising and marketing campaign is to revisit your market research. Ask yourself these questions one more time:

- *Who are my potential customers?* (Restaurants, specialty markets, garden centers, crafters, tourists, or some other group entirely?)

- *How many are there?*

- *Where are they located?*

- *Where do they now find the products I want to provide?*

- *What can I offer that they're not already getting from this other source?*

- *How can I persuade them to purchase my herbs or herbal products?*

Look over the answers to these questions—then ask yourself some more:

- *What knowledge and skills am I offering?*

- *What image do I want to project?*

- *How do I compare with my competition, and how can I be better?*

After you've answered these questions, you can start planning your strategy and the type of advertising you'll do.

Special Delivery

Direct mail can be one of the herbal entrepreneur's best advertising tools—for two reasons. First, it gives you the ability to sell to customers all over the country, or all over the world if you choose, whether your herb business is tucked deep in the North Woods of Michigan, outside a tiny town in the Mississippi Delta, or in any other rural, off-the-beaten-track locale. Second, direct mail lets you target the specific market you want to attract. Because you send your sales piece right into the mailboxes of potential customers with a proven interest in your type of products, you eliminate the problem of spending advertising dollars on people who don't fit your niche.

If you plan to sell fresh-cut herbs to restaurant chefs, for instance, you can send sales letters or fliers to every restaurant on the upscale west side of town, only establishments with entrees priced over $18, or whatever eateries fit your particular market strategy.

For dried herb mixes or potted culinary herbs you want to sell to home cooks, you can send catalogs to people who already subscribe to cooking magazines or cook book clubs—potential customers who already have a track record of buying cooking-related products by mail.

OK, so where do you find all those home chefs for your herbs, home gardeners to buy your hand-milled gardener's soap, or parents to purchase your kids' soothing sleep pillows—or whatever it is you're selling? As we briefly explored in Chapter 4, you've got several sources:

- *Directories from clubs, civic and professional organizations, nonprofit associations, or other groups*
- *List brokers*
- *Your own in-house lists*

Directory Information

You may already belong to a group that's the perfect target market for your herbal products—think culinary societies for those cooking herbs; gardening clubs for that gardener's hand soap; or parents' groups ranging from the PTA to home-school associations for your sleep pillows. If your organization is a local one, that's great. But if it has regional or national chapters, so much the better. More names!

Just Listed

As an added bonus to compiling your own mailing list, you can make money with it without selling a single product. You do this by offering your list through a broker in exchange for a commission, usually about 20 percent of your rental fee. So if you charge the going rate of $50 per thousand names and a company that sells garden tools, for instance, buys 10,000 names, you earn $500. Pay the broker a $100 commission, and the other $400 is yours!

The fear that another herbal products company will usurp your popularity and "steal" your customers is generally groundless. Customers who buy one brand of product will more likely than not buy another brand as well. A little competition is a good thing!

▲

Smart Tip

Tip...

Why not swap mailing lists with another cooking, gardening, or herb-oriented company? Choose a business whose products are different but of interest to the same type of customers, then exchange lists, either as a one-time deal or a permanent trade.

If your products are designed for a more general market, like herbal spa bath kits for the chronically busy (and who isn't these days?), then you might start off with any associations you belong to, be they car club, pony club, quilters' guild, weight-loss group or teachers' league.

The main point here is that you've probably already got a membership directory filled with potential customers' names stashed in your kitchen catch-all drawer or buried somewhere in that "To Be Filed" file in your home office. If not, you may be able to beg, borrow, or buy a directory from the organization's main office.

Brainstorm any other associations whose membership rosters you may be able to get access to, including those of your spouse or significant other; your siblings, parents and children; and any other friends or relatives who might be willing to contribute a mailing list.

Be sure to consider church groups, client lists, employee directories, neighborhood groups, fraternal organizations like the Elks Lodge, alumni associations, and sororities and fraternities. And don't neglect your own address book—you've probably got far more names and addresses scribbled in there than you realize.

Going for Brokers

Perhaps one of the best sources of mailing lists is the list broker, a person (or perhaps more accurately, a company) whose only business is developing and renting out names and addresses. List brokers can supply you with lists for just about every specialty imaginable—cooking, gardening, crafts, home décor, kids, parents, grandparents, travelers, asthmatics, arthritis sufferers, working women, athletic men, and much, much more.

Even better, a good list broker can pull together specific criteria, called "selects," to best target your particular market. Say you're selling herbal apothecaries for kids. Your market research has shown that college-educated moms with a household income of more than $50,000 per year are most likely to purchase your products. You want to start your sales blitz on a relatively small scale by sending catalogs to potential customers in part of your state instead of nationwide, so you request a list consisting of names of college-educated

Smart Tip

Tip...

Find a farmers' market in your state by clicking on www.ams.usda.gov/farmers markets/.

moms with annual household incomes of $50,000-plus who have preteen kids and live in Southern California.

Where does the list broker get all these names? They come from all sorts of sources, including magazine subscriptions, the cards you fill out and mail in when you register a new piece of software or a new refrigerator,

Smart Tip

While you're out and about on your herbal business, collect business cards of people you meet. They can be valuable additions to your in-house list.

financial ratings lists, rosters of political and professional organizations, and the customer lists of other companies who sell by mail order.

All these lovely names come with a price tag, of course. Costs vary depending on how many selects you request and the type of list you rent. A *compiled* list for the purveyor of culinary herbs for home chefs, for instance, might be composed of people who subscribe to gourmet magazines. A *response* list, however, would consist of people who not only subscribe to gourmet magazines and earn more than $60,000 annually but have also purchased cooking products by mail in the past six months. The latter bit of information is important because it tells you that they're quite likely to buy your products instead of tossing your catalog into the trash.

As you might have guessed, a response list is more expensive than a compiled one. Expect to pay about $50 per 1,000 names for the latter, as compared to as much as $120 per 1,000 names for the response list, plus $5 to $10 extra for each select—like age, income, or geographic region—that you request. And list brokers generally demand that you rent at least 3,000 to 5,000 names at a time.

We say "rent" instead of "purchase" because you only get to use each list once. If you want to use the list again, you pay another rental fee. The exception to this rule is that any names who respond to your mailing are yours to keep and reuse as often as you like, absolutely free.

Making a List

That brings us to the third option for finding direct-mail customers: your own in-house list. You should begin developing a company mailing list at about the same time you start developing your business—it's never too soon to start. Try these tips for building your own list:

- *Use the names you receive in response to your market research surveys.*
- *Keep a guest book with spaces for visitors to record their names and addresses.* Ask people to write in it when you host your grand opening party, as well as any other business or shop events.
- *Prominently display a guest book at your sales counter or table with a sign that invites customers to join your mailing list and receive herbal newsletters and/or "preferred customer" notifications of sales and events.*

- *Request that people who attend your seminars and workshops complete a post-event evaluation form—which includes space for their names and addresses.*

While you're merrily adding these names to your list, don't neglect to maintain it. Make sure you've got each name entered only once—sending duplicate sales materials not only looks unprofessional but is also a serious waste of money. Weed out any nixies—those return-to-sender names—and edit any that notify you of new addresses. Make sure, too, that you've entered all names and addresses correctly into your database. Nobody likes to get a piece of mail with their name spelled wrong, and sending mail to a nonexistent address is pound, and penny-foolish.

Letter Perfect

Now that you've got a mailing list and you're ready to sell, what's next? Designing sales materials that do the job is your next task. If you've done your homework and thoroughly researched your market, then developed herbal products your target audience wants, your job is far easier. But you must still persuade your potential customers that they want what you've got to offer.

The rules are the same whether you go with a flier, brochure, catalog, or sales letter. Choose whichever matches your company's style and ambiance, then use your imagination to reach out to your potential customers, along with these tips:

- *Write as though you're sending a personal note to one special customer—not as if you're sending the same message to everyone on your mailing list (even though you are).* Let your excitement about your herbs and herbal products come through.

- *When possible, use magic words like "secret" and "free."* Everybody wants to know a secret, and everybody wants something for free! Try something like: "Learn the secrets of cooking with fresh herbs instead of fats and salt!" or "Free planting guide when you buy six or more potted herbs!"

- *Don't skimp on words.* Surprisingly, even though people complain about the profusion of junk mail they receive, longer sells better than shorter. People in your target market are interested in what you're selling; you know that already. So indulge their interests—tell them all about your botanicals or other herbal products.

- *Use indented paragraphs, boldface type, italics, underlined words, and two colors—*they pack more of a punch and pull out plain text. But use these tactics sparingly. Overused, they lose their impact and become downright annoying.

- *Make sure all spelling, grammar, and punctuation is perfect.* Even if you're a former high school English teacher, have a trusted colleague or relative look over your materials. You could miss something just by having read it too often.

Bright Idea

Add value to your herbs by creating your own teaching—and marketing—materials, as well as your own products. "I am in the process of creating [a new] catalog, a new booklet called "Ten Herbs You Must Have In Your Garden," gift baskets, and who knows what else!" says Michele B. in Soddy Daisy, Tennessee.

Expert Testimony

One of the herbal entrepreneur's most effective direct-mail tools is the testimonial. This is a quote from a customer praising your products. You've seen them before, things like "I have a lot less headaches since using your lavender and mint light ring diffuser. Thank you!"—*Cindy Sanders, St. Louis.*" It may seem cornball, but it works. Other people's favorable reviews add considerable credence to your own claims of excellence. If you say your product is great, you're advertising. But if a customer says it's great, it probably is.

How do you get testimonials? Just ask. When satisfied customers call, write or e-mail with a compliment, ask if you can use that quote in your promotional materials. Most people are flattered to be asked and will readily agree. Write up their comment and send it to them with a request for a permission signature. Or send customers questionnaires about your products and then ask permission to use the most favorable and interesting ones as testimonials (keep in mind that it's illegal to use them without permission). You might sprinkle testimonials from various customers throughout your catalog or add a page of them to a sales letter.

News from the Farm

Many herb entrepreneurs choose to go with a variation on the direct-mail theme, the newsletter, to promote their products. Ralph C. in Elizabethtown, Pennsylvania, sends one out to new and existing customers every month during summer growing

By Request

Donna F. started selling her dried herb mixes via mail order "by request." She lives in an area in Midland, Michigan, where residents are frequently transferred out of state. When those folks began calling, asking for the products they'd been buying from her at the farmers' market, Donna put together a trifold brochure that serves as a minicatalog.

The catalog serves another purpose as well: Donna hands it out at the farmers' market to customers who want additional recipes and mix ideas.

season and every other month the rest of the year. "My customers look forward to dropping everything and reading it," Ralph says. "It reminds them that we're here, and it puts my current price list in front of them."

Ralph originally considered a color catalog, but when he compared the huge expenses incurred in putting out a glossy, full-color production with the relatively minor cost of a simple newsletter, he went with the latter. Catalogs are too expensive, he says, and after they're printed, your prices can change, rendering the whole thing out of date.

The decorative herb and flower grower keeps his newsletter folksy and humorous. "Sometimes I write it like a grouchy old man," Ralph admits—to the delight of his customers.

Some herb newsletters describe seasonal changes in the garden and give monthly planting tips and seasonal recipes. Others deliver snippets of herbal lore or calendars of lectures, festivals, and other events on the farm. Tailor your newsletter, to your own style and your farm's ambiance.

Cataloging Profits

Catalogs don't have to be giant, glossy, four-color productions, nor should they be—not unless and until you've got a market you feel will duly compensate you for the cost. Those sleek magazines put out by companies like garden experts Smith & Hawken are gorgeous—and very expensive. Fancy photography and printing come with hefty price tags.

As an herbal entrepreneur, you don't have to go that route. Instead of slick and glossy, you might aim for the personal touch, portraying yourself as the herb expert who's small enough to be friendly and accessible. Use your imagination and design your catalog on back-to-nature craft paper with just one or two ink colors, then sprinkle liberally with tips, recipes, and herbal lore. Tailor your topics to the season, as well as to the products within your pages, and your customers will eagerly await each "issue."

Bright Idea
Stash a percent-off coupon into your catalog. Specify certain plants or products that are reaching the end of the season or haven't sold well—it's a good way to encourage sales, as well as liquidate stock.

Taking Orders

No matter whether your catalog is a 48-page full-color extravaganza or a simple 12-page work on recycled paper, the order form will be one of its most important elements. Don't make it hard to find! Instead of hiding it at the back of the book as an afterthought, print it on different colored paper or different stock and bind it right into the center of the catalog.

Since not everybody wants to send in a form, print your phone number, fax number, and Web site address on the form and in the catalog as well, along with an invitation to order by those methods.

Bright Idea

Leave a section for customers to fill in the name and address of a friend who might like to receive your catalog—then add that information to your mailing list.

Leave plenty of space on your order form for customers to fill in all necessary information, including the following:

- *Customer's name, address, phone number, and e-mail address*
- *Item number and description (including size and color if applicable)*
- *Quantity*
- *Price per item*
- *Item price total*
- *Gift box or wrapping (if applicable)—don't forget to charge extra for this service*
- *Space for gift mailing address*
- *Subtotal price of all items*
- *Sales tax, clearly described*
- *Shipping charges, clearly described*
- *Total order price*
- *Payment method with room for credit card information, including account number, expiration date, and cardholder's name*
- *Your return policy, clearly spelled out*
- *A nice thank-you for the order*

The Web Garden

When you put up a Web site, customers can access your garden 24/7, even while you're out in the garden planting or harvesting, making your delivery rounds, or working the farmers' market. They can ask questions via e-mail, read your online newsletters, share or request recipes, and, of course, order products. "I sell quite a bit over the Internet," says Cindy M. in Hallettsville, Texas. "My Web site has proven to be a great sales tool not only for out-of-town business but also for local people to learn about [my farm]."

▲

Smart Tip

Tip...

Check out competitors' Web sites, just as you check out competitors' other advertising materials. Borrow the best of what they're doing, then do it better. It never hurts to order a plant or product or two from them either, to see exactly what's delivered and how.

Michele B. in Soddy Daisy, Tennessee, has also found her Web site to be a boon—augmented by other advertising avenues. "Right now we advertise through the *Herb Companion* [a print magazine], the Herb Growing and Marketing Network, garden Web sites and search engines, links through other herb and gardening businesses, articles in local newspapers, and public service announcements on local radio and TV. She says, "I hand out business cards whenever I can and often provide a little leaflet that has herbal info on it to whoever asks."

Her most successful avenues? She says the Herb Growing and Marketing Network site and her own Web site have gotten the word out the best. "[I get] lots of response from that," she says, "at least 80 percent."

Mike R. in Sequim, Washington, agrees a Web site is the way to go. "I don't advertise in the newspaper at all," he says. "It's never panned out. We're getting hundreds and hundreds of hits on our Web site, and it costs $20. Why would I go out and advertise in the paper to get two or three inquiries?"

The Personal Touch

Customers who surf and shop the Net tend to be more adventurous than traditional shoppers, which makes them good candidates for new herbs and herbal products. But like direct-mail customers, they want the personal touch. Even if they're surfing your site from across the country at 3 in the morning, they want to feel that you know them. Give 'em what they crave with these virtual tips:

- *Be available for questions, comments, and orders.* Don't force customers to wade through page after page before finding your e-mail address and phone number.

- *Check and answer your e-mail on a daily basis.* The faster you respond, the more likely you are to get orders.

- *Update your site frequently.* Change prices when necessary and add new tips, tidbits, recipes, or crafts often. This keeps customers coming back for more and provides new reasons to purchase products.

- *Keep your site user-friendly and easy to navigate instead of slow and complicated—and go easy on the graphics.* Pictures add impact to your site, but if your customers have to wait seemingly endless minutes for your page to become viewable because it's graphics-heavy, you're going to lose them. Make sure those photos are small enough to load quickly.

Calling All Herbs

Whether you conduct your "mail order" business by mail or online, you'll get phone calls from customers. Some people feel that placing an order by telephone is faster and safer than ordering by mail or Internet. Others want to ask questions about products before making a purchase. In any case, the way you answer calls can spell either sales success or disaster. Follow these tips for phone sales achievement:

- *Be of good cheer.* Always answer in a pleasant, cheerful tone. Even if it's been raining buckets for days, your garden is turning into a lake, and the dog just ate your carefully crafted herb wreaths, your customer should hear a confident, happy voice. Don't forget to answer with your company name, not just "hello."

- *Ask for details.* Make sure you know what your customer is ordering. If you carry several varieties of potted rosemary, for instance, ask which one the customer wants. If you stock "Thyme for Tea" T-shirts in different sizes or colors, ask for particulars. Repeat all ordering information to be certain you've got it right. This will not only prevent an unhappy customer, but it will also save you a refund or exchange.

- *Ad info.* Ask how your customer learned about your herb business—if in an ad, in what publication? This is an important way to determine which advertising venues pay off.

- *Upsell.* Upselling, or suggesting additional plants or other purchases, is a terrific sales tool that works better than you might imagine. Read more about it in "The Power of Suggestion" on page 152.

- *Address, please.* Get your customer's name, address, phone number, and e-mail address; then read it back to make sure you've got it right. Keep in mind that FedEx and UPS can't deliver to a post office box, so you'll need a physical address if you use those services.

- *Get the gift of goods.* Find out if your customer would like that starter set of herbs or baby-welcoming wreath shipped to someone else as a gift; then get that address.

- *Will that be all?* Ask if your customer would like to order anything else. It makes her stop and think—and sometimes answer yes! It also makes you sound interested in continuing the conversation instead of abruptly ending it.

- *Get paid.* Take your customer's credit card information—you'll need the account number, expiration date, and cardholder's name.

Bright Idea

Send a token gift along with that order—anything from a packet of seeds to a few recipe cards. Customers appreciate the freebie and feel like you've singled them out for a gift— which encourages repeat sales.

▲

- *Ship 'em out.* Tell your customers when the order will be shipped and when they can expect it to arrive. If they're ordering live plants, explain that they'll come with planting instructions.

- *Appreciate.* Thank your customers for their order and encourage them to call again. Repeat customers are your best source of sales, so make them feel appreciated.

Fit to Print

Print ads, the ones you find in newspapers and magazines, are not the cheapest way to promote your herb business and its products, but they can be effective—if used wisely. Before proceeding, first and foremost, you need to decide if your target market is local, regional, or national.

If you plan to sell potted herbs or herb crafts to local residents and tourists, for instance, you could advertise in a national publication like *Country Living* magazine. But it would be a waste of money. The readership is way too broad, you'd have no assurance that local gardeners or crafters were being reached, and the price would make a major dent in your budget. Even a small ad in a national publication can run as high as $3,500 and up.

However, you could advertise in your local newspaper for as little as $60 to $100. This way, you'd know readers were in your town instead of spread all over the country.

The Power of Suggestion

Cross-selling and upselling are great ways to encourage customers to purchase additional items. And it's not as difficult as it might sound—after all, your customer has called to place an order, which means he's interested in your products. It also means he'll most likely be flattered when you suggest something else—showing that you're interested enough in him to consider what else he might want.

So how do you do it? First, upsell by offering that customer a special on two or more products of the same type. If he's ordering a Renaissance Remedy Garden collection, for instance, offer a Mediterranean Cook's Garden collection as well for 10% off.

You can also cross-sell by offering your customer a product related to the one he's purchasing. If he's ordering that Mediterranean Cook's Garden, for instance, suggest your Mediterranean Herb Magic cookbook to go with it. Explain—so long as it's true, of course—that your customers who order one are usually delighted with the other.

And if you advertised in the garden or lifestyle section, you could be fairly certain you were reaching gardeners and crafters.

Getting the word out about herbs or herbal products sold by mail order, or even tours of your display gardens and shop, requires a different strategy. Because your customer base will be much broader, advertising in a national publication may make sense. Or you might choose to advertise in a regional edition of a national magazine, targeting, for instance, gardeners only in the South. This can help you reach a narrower target market while still going with a big-name national publication, and ad prices will be lower.

A Fine Display

Whether you choose magazines or newspapers, print ads come in one of two styles: *classified* and *display*. Display ads usually feature some sort of graphics combined with the printed word and are found throughout a publication. Classifieds consist solely of the printed word and are found only in the classified section.

Take a look at the sample display ad on the next page. This is called a two-step ad because prospective customers must take two steps to purchase—first they have to request the catalog and then order. What's the advantage over the one-step ad, which includes prices for specific products and an order form?

- *You know that readers who respond are interested*—after all, they've taken the time and effort to request a catalog. And they pay for the catalog, which nicely offsets its mailing cost.

- *You get names of respondents to add to your mailing list.*

Note that readers are tempted to shop and then purchase with the promise of a free gift, which can be as simple as a packet of recipe cards, an envelope of seeds ,or a minibundle of herbs. You needn't offer a freebie; instead, you could offer a discount on their first purchase.

Classified Information

Classified ads are far less expensive than display ads, but they're also riskier. Since people generally only turn to the classifieds when they're looking for something in particular, and then only look in that specific section, you run the risk that the casual reader

Sample Display Ad

Thyme Out Herb Farm

Heirloom Herb Plants
Fragrant Herb Bundles, Dream Pillows, Wreaths & Potpourri
Herbal Awareness Gift Baskets—Give Someone You Love the Gift of Time

Visit us online or send $2 for our Thyme Out catalog, brimming with herbal lore to help tune your hectic modern life to the rhythm of the seasons.

Ask for your free gift with your first order!

168 Thyme Creek Road, Cottage Garden, GA 40500
(440) 555-6100   www.thymeoutherbs.com

will pass them by entirely. Take a look at the sample classified ad opposite. It's also a two-step ad. Note that all extraneous words have been culled to keep the per-word price to a minimum. While brevity may seem tacky in a display ad, it's expected in the classifieds. Just don't get so brief that you leave out important items like your contact information.

Talk of the Town

No matter what other advertising and marketing measures you take, nothing sells like people talking about your products. Wholesale or retail customers who are happy with your culinary, health, beauty, or crafts products will tell their friends and colleagues, who then also become customers who spread the word.

"Word of mouth is the best advertising in my small community," says Cindy M., who takes advantage of a variety of different

Tip...

Smart Tip

Don't limit your speaking engagements to local civic groups. Give talks at herb industry conferences as well. "We speak at all conferences," says Mike R. in Sequim, Washington. "We're registered with the Herb Growing and Marketing Network Speakers Bureau. We speak for a very inexpensive fee, but we get lots of exposure."

Sample Classified Ad

Take THYME OUT with our special herbs.

Tune hectic modern life to rhythm of the seasons with our heirloom plants, potpourri, dream pillows, baskets, wreaths.

Catalog $2.

Free gift with first order!

Thyme Out Herb Farm,
168 Thyme Creek Rd., Cottage Garden, GA 40500
(404) 555-6100   www.thymeoutherbs.com

promotional techniques. "I run ads in the local newspaper during peak season. I show up at local events with my plants. I advertise with a local RV park, and I have a road-side sign that attracts a certain number of people just out for a ride in the country. I also advertise my services as a speaker for clubs, libraries, and the like. This helps introduce targeted audiences to my herbs and broadens their view of how herbs can be used.

"Word of mouth—customers bringing friends and relatives out to the nursery—is probably my best advertising venue because, in a way, it's free. Also, showing up at local events puts a face on my business, and locally, that's very important."

Who Ya Gonna Call?

While word-of-mouth advertising is indeed free, that doesn't mean it happens automatically. Like Cindy, you have to actively work at it. You won't find customers by perching in the garden waiting for the phone to ring. You have to get out and meet people, or in other parlance, network.

"Maintain a high profile," advises Ralph C., who joined not only the Herb Growers and Marketers Network but also the Association of Specialty Cut Flowers—and became a board member. As a board member or even a volunteer on various committees, you become a voice in the industry. When other growers need to buy extra herbs or

Tip...

Smart Tip

Look for shows sponsored by local industry associations, then attend them and mingle, advises Cindy M. in Hallettsville, Texas. "I sell at shows sponsored by the Texas Herb Growers and Marketers Association. These are generally well-attended by people looking specifically for herbs and unusual plants—and they're a great way to make connections with other growers."

want to refer customers to someone who grows herbs that they don't, you're the one they call.

If your competitors want to know a trade secret—like where you found a certain seed—and they'll discover the answer for themselves anyway, go ahead and tell them, Ralph advises. Then when you want information from them, they feel more inclined to tell you. "I can call hundreds of people and ask for assistance," the cut flower and herb purveyor says. "It's the old karma thing—you get what you give." It's also terrific word-of-mouth marketing.

And it goes on and on. Be nice to the UPS delivery man, and he just might suggest that a gift shop customer call you about your products. Practice kindness with your employees, and they'll brag to everyone about where they work. "Being a nice guy helps," Ralph says. "It rarely comes back to haunt me."

Pressing Matters

Ralph C.'s herb and flower business has graced the pages of *Martha Stewart Living* magazine, and Mike and Jadyne R.'s lavender business has appeared in articles in half a dozen magazines in nearly as many years. How did they do it?

Exposure. The more exposure you give your business, the more successful it's likely to become. And while the owners of these businesses didn't set out specifically to woo

Well-Spoken

Speaking engagements are a terrific way to promote your herbal products without spending a lot of money. In fact, as your name and fame grow, you can charge money for seminars and workshops.

Start off by generously donating your herbal expertise to all sorts of local groups. Everybody from junior colleges to the chamber of commerce to the library is hungry for speakers for their meetings and other events. When you step in as a pro bono, or free, guest speaker, they're delighted. And you garner that priceless word-of-mouth advertising.

Tailor your talks to your audience. You might, for instance, discuss cooking with herbs in place of salt for a health group, explore herbs as ground cover instead of grass for the local men's club, give low-fat herbal cooking tips to a weight-loss group, and talk about medieval physick gardens to a book club or library group.

Smart Tip

Tip...

Discover everything you'll need to know to be a seminar and workshop pro with Entrepreneur's business start-up guide, *Start Your Own Seminar Production Business*.

the editors of the magazines they appeared in, one bit of press led to another until they got noticed.

You can do the same. Send news releases (which are also called press releases) to local and regional publications each time you host an event at your business or shop, start selling a new and interesting herb or herbal product, donate products to charity, or give a talk or workshop. Even when you don't have something new to trumpet, you can write a release that ties your products in to current events.

News releases take the form of one- or two-page articles, accompanied by a photo of your product. Take a look at the sample news release on page 158, then try these tips for news release success:

- *Craft your release to sound like news instead of advertising.* Editors want to read and publish hard copy—their purpose isn't to give you a free plug.

- *Keep your release short and concise with a cutting edge of interest.* Tailor a news release, for instance, about your lavender and thyme plants—herbs with antiseptic properties—to tie in with current concerns about the cold and flu season.

- *Customize your release to the publication.* Write a release on new culinary herb trends for cooking magazines; tweak it to emphasize the benefits of herbs instead of salt for a health publication or a magazine for seniors.

- *Follow the standard news release format.* Start off with a catchy lead, or opening, followed by hard but fascinating facts. Double-space your copy. Keep your font easy to read—this is not the place to experiment with quirky typefaces.

- *Call the magazine and ask to which editor your release should be addressed.* It won't do to send a story on soothing teas for toddlers to the automotive editor. Get correct name spellings and addresses.

- *Follow up.* Wait a few weeks, then call the editor to make sure she's received the release and ask if she has any questions. Then be persistent—if your first release doesn't make it to print, try again with a new one.

In addition to press releases, volunteer to write articles or columns for local and regional publications. You'll soon become known as an expert, and your herb business will gain lots of valuable exposure.

Bright Idea

Cooking tips sell. Put together a set of recipe cards featuring types of dishes—soups, stews, salads, entrees, desserts, etc.—all using herbs. Design an herb cookery booklet. Or write a full-fledged cookbook of recipes from your farm.

Sample News Release

Thyme Out Herb Farm

For Immediate Release: Contact: Sorrel Seabrook
                                                    (440) 555-6100

With the holiday season upon us, most families will be embarking on that over-the-river-and-through-the-snow journey to Grandma's or other relatives' homes. But how to travel with overexcited small children who often succumb to fretfulness on long car or air trips? If you're a mom or dad, you know this can be a major problem.

But there are simple, healthy, and time-honored solutions, says Sorrel Seabrook of Thyme Out Herb Farm in Cottage Garden, Georgia. That cranky toddler who refuses to sleep on the plane can be soothed with a Carlyle Cuddle Bunny, a snuggly chenille rabbit stuffed with chamomile, hops, lemon balm, and lavender. The aromatic qualities of these child-safe herbs, from sachet-scented lavender to pleasantly apple-scented chamomile, are soothing and help send overstimulated tots to nap nirvana.

Tots can also be lured into lullaby land with a few drops of Lullaby Lavender essential oil placed on a parent's sweater to cuddle into or on baby's blanket. And older kids can take a snooze break from highway bingo with Thyme Out's lavender and lemon balm Dreamtime Pillow.

Herbal remedies such as these have been used for centuries, says Seabrook, but pediatricians and other physicians have only recently rediscovered their benefits.

Carlyle Cuddle Bunny, Lullaby Lavender essential oil, and Dreamtime Pillows are available from Thyme Out Herb Farm.

168 Thyme Creek Road,
Cottage Garden, GA 40500
(440) 555-6100
www.thymeoutherbs.com

Making a Mint
Controlling Your Finances

Just as your herbs need periodic checkups to make sure they've got the glow of health, so do your finances. If you don't keep careful track of expenses going out, as well as earnings coming in, you won't know if you're in the green or being eaten alive by operating costs until you reach the panic point of losing the farm.

Financial checkups can reveal that you're spending too much on direct-mail advertising or on the trappings and treats at herb festivals. Or they can divulge that you're doing great, that you can now afford to take on summer help in the greenhouse or build that little shop next to the driveway. If you discover, after carefully penciling in your costs, that you're not going to be able to afford that fancy new John Deere tractor this year, don't reach for the triple-strength infusion of St. John's wort. Take a breath instead.

Keep in mind that the first years in the life of your business are generally the most expensive. You've had all those setup costs, from buying a greenhouse—or even your land—and purchasing plants, soil amendments, and equipment to registering your business name. Those are all one-time expenses, so life should get easier once they are paid off and out of the way.

Of course, herb farmers are always saving to set up another, larger greenhouse, add more plant stock, and perhaps even create that cute shop or tearoom. But those don't have to happen right away. You can take your time and let your income grow along with your herbs before branching out.

Staying on Course

An *income and expense statement*, also called a *profit-and-loss statement*, charts the revenues and operating costs of your business over a specific period of time. For a peek at what it looks like and how to go about creating one for your business, check out the income statements on pages 161 and 162 for our two hypothetical herb businesses, Sage Advice and Herban Planet.

You'll want to tailor your income statement to your particular business. Use the worksheet on page 163 to chart your own income statement. Then sit back for a moment and smell the rosemary.

Feeding Uncle Sam

There's another hungry mouth to consider besides the caterpillars looking to bite off a chunk of your herb business, and that's Uncle Sam. While you should consult your accountant for the details as they pertain to your specific business, many small ventures can figure on a few basics when it comes to tax time.

You can, for example, deduct a percentage of your home office so long as you're using it solely as an office. These deductions include all normal office expenses plus interest, taxes,

Smart Tip

Contrary to popular belief, the IRS can be nice—at least if you just want a question or two answered. Go online at www.irs.gov to find the toll-free number for your region, then give them a ring.

Sample Income and Expense Statement

Sage Advise Herb Farm

INCOME & EXPENSE STATEMENT
For the Year Ending December 31, 2002

Income

Retail potted herbs	$26,617.50

Expenses

Rent	$0
Phone/utilities	1,260
Electronic card processing	300
Employees	0
Misc. postage	240
Licenses	96
Legal services	360
Accounting services	300
Office supplies	120
Advertising	500
Web hosting	360
Internet service	240
Soil/pots	400
Seeds/stock	200
Farmers' market fees	100
Auto expenses	500
Loan repayment	0
Miscellaneous	470

Total Expenses	**(−5,446.00)**
Net Annual Income	**$21,171.50**

Note: Shipping supplies and mailing costs are not shown here as they're charged to mail-order customers.

Sample Income and Expense Statement

Herban Planet

INCOME & EXPENSE STATEMENT
For the Year Ending December 31, 2002

Income
Fresh-cut herb sales	$35,425
Herb craft sales	38,480

Gross Income	73,905

Cost of Sales
Crafts materials & supplies	(−19,921)
(includes essential oils, soap bases, wreath frames, ribbons, bottles, and packaging)	

Expenses
Rent	$0
Phone/utilities	1,200
Employees	0
Postage	240
Licenses	96
Legal services	360
Accounting services	300
Office supplies	120
Advertising	800
Web hosting	360
Internet service	240
Soil/pots	200
Seeds/stock	200
Auto expenses	1,000
Loan repayment	1,260
Miscellaneous	533

Total Expenses	**(−6,913)**

Net Annual Income	**$47,071**

Your Income and Expense Statement

For the Year Ending _____

Income $_____

Expenses

   Phone/utilities   _____

   Electronic card processing   _____

   Employees   _____

   Postage   _____

   Licenses   _____

   Legal services   _____

   Accounting services   _____

   Office supplies   _____

   Internet service   _____

   Web hosting   _____

   Loan repayment   _____

   Miscellaneous   _____

Total Expenses   (-_____)

Net Annual Income $_____

insurance, and depreciation on the portion of the house used as an office. This can get complicated—the total amount of the deduction is limited by the gross income you derive from the business activity minus all your other business expenses apart from those related to the home office.

Besides your office, you can deduct business-related phone calls, the cost of business equipment and supplies (again, so long as you're truly using them solely for your business), subscriptions to professional and trade journals, and auto expenses. Keep a log of business miles to deduct for deliveries, trips to speaking engagements, and runs to the nursery supply center.

You can also deduct entertainment expenses like that grand opening party, midsummer or Christmas open house, or even a dinner for a visiting wholesaler whose

Tip...

Smart Tip

If you're not doing as well as you'd like, advises herb grower and herb association vice president Cindy M. in Hallettsville, Texas, be flexible. Look at your business honestly and see whether you're offering what people want. Don't be afraid to alter what you're doing. Add products or change your advertising—whatever it takes.

business you're courting. Be sure, though, to keep a diary of all these expenses, especially if they come to under $75 a pop (you don't technically need to keep receipts for these), and if you're entertaining at home, have your customers sign a guest book.

And remember that you must have a business-related purpose for entertaining. General goodwill toward potential customers or sales reps doesn't cut it, so be sure your diary contains the reason for the partying.

When you travel for business purposes, you can deduct air fares, train tickets, and rental car mileage along with hotels and meals. And you can even—under certain circumstances—deduct recreational side trips you take with your family while you're traveling on business. Since the IRS allows deductions for any such trip you take to expand your awareness and expertise in your field of business, it makes sense to also take advantage of any conferences or seminars that you can attend while on holiday to keep abreast of events in your target market or to see how the competition's doing.

Seeing Green

As a savvy herb entrepreneur, you've got a variety of options for increasing your income. One way is to host open houses and fairs, terrific venues for promoting your products while building goodwill. By inviting customers to tour your display gardens, sample your edible products, or participate in craftable ones, you make people feel like a part of your herb family—which in turn encourages sales.

Make your party a simple open house—like your grand opening—with free noshes and lots of herbal wares on display for purchase. Or turn it into an all-day event with crafts workshops, culinary classes, and herb lectures as well.

Get creative and dream up ideas like these:

- *Midsummer Faerie Festival.* Everyone knows flowers, fairies and herbs go together. Invite customers to sample dainty herbal tea party fare, craft fairy nosegays and fairy abodes of fresh herbs and twigs, and design greeting cards from dried herbal flowers and snippets of verse from "A Midsummer Night's Dream."

- *Harvest Moon Evening Faire.* Celebrate the harvest under a full moon with herbal autumn edibles and crafts workshops on making autumn bounty

On Tour

Get away from the business every now and then to visit other herb farms, advises Ralph C. in Elizabethtown, Pennsylvania. Weekend trips to other growers are terrific opportunities to pick up on new techniques, as well as make friends and contacts in the industry.

Don't be shy. Choose a grower in the area you want to visit, Ralph suggests. Then place a call and ask if you can take a tour. You'll find that other herb farmers are eager to show you around, and you'll learn more than you might expect—and have fun!

wreaths, pumpkin herb centerpieces, and end-of-summer garden scrapbooks.

- *Herbal Christmas Celebration.* Go all out with workshops on crafting herbal gifts and decorations. Don't forget to set out herb-infused snacks and libations for all those elves who'll attend the event.

- *Spring Seedling Garden Party.* Take advantage of spring fever by setting out seeds, seedlings, and pots to plant them in. Customers can participate in workshops on decorating pots and other planting containers or learn to design their own herb gardens.

Although a simple open house should be free, workshops and other events should carry a price tag. Perhaps surprisingly, people willingly pay the same—or more—to assemble their own topiaries or other herbal crafts as they do to buy the finished product. After all, they're learning, as well as benefiting from the joy of creativity—and they're getting encouragement from you in the process. Most people don't have a lot of confidence in their creative capabilities (and lots don't have any imagination to dream up projects, either). But you're an expert, and your guidance and reassurance will make a tremendous difference not only in the finished product but in how they feel about it.

Keep in mind, too, that for every wreath, herb garden in a pot, or other project customers craft, there are likely several more they'll want to make on their own—which means they'll buy the materials, whether dried botanicals, starter plants, or whatever, from you. And each time they step into your garden or shop to purchase those materials, they'll probably buy something else as well.

Make your fairs or open houses annual events. Send out invitations with reservation forms for workshops to alert and remind customers. You'll find that soon they're asking you about the next party date.

▲

In the Workshop

Besides pulling out all the stops and throwing a full-fledged party as the seasons change, you can also host make-it-yourself workshops on a monthly basis, or whatever frequency suits your schedule and your customers' whims. Encourage customers to attend on their own, with a garden club, as a mother-daughter event, or as a birthday or holiday treat for a friend.

Design a yearly calendar of events and make lots of copies to hand out with purchases, as well as to mail with newsletters, fliers, and other promotional pieces. Then start taking payments for reservations. Make sure you charge enough to cover your materials. If your workshop will feature making a Thanksgiving herb centerpiece, for instance, you'll want to figure the cost of a basket, botanicals, ribbons, glue or florist's wire, and any other materials. Even though the herbs will probably come from your own farm, you'll need to charge retail prices.

Add in the cost of any fees you'll pay to guest experts or employees to teach the class. If your expert charges you $60, for instance, and you plan to have 15 participants,

Sample Workshop Pricing

Workshop Project: Thanksgiving Herb Centerpiece

Material		Retail Price
(1) Styrofoam block		$ 0.99
(1) Bundle sweet annie		2.95
(2) Sage starter		5.00
(1) Thyme starter		2.50
(3) Baby pumpkins		2.75
(1) Bayberry candle		4.95
Materials total		$19.14
Expert's fee or employee wages	$60.00	
Divide by number of expected participants	15	
Fee or wage total		4.00
Total Cost of Workshop Per Participant		$23.14

Note: Your total costs come to $23.14, which is a weird figure for most people to absorb. You'll make a smidgen of profit per participant—and participants will be happier—if you charge a flat $25 for each attendee.

add a cost of $4 per customer (60 divided by 15) onto your workshop price. Take a look at the sample pricing worksheet on page 166, then make up your own using the blank form below.

Most customers will be eager to attend your events, but there will always be some who flake out at the last minute. Develop a cancellation policy and spell it out on your annual event schedule, as well as any other event materials. A smart way to deal with this problem is to allow refunds if you're notified of a cancellation up to a week or 10 days in advance of the event. This gives you time to fill empty spots, as well as to collect the materials you'll need.

Let customers know that cancellations received after your cutoff date cannot be refunded. If you like, you can offer to give cancellers workshop materials to take home or a seat at another similarly priced event.

Be My Guest

Another nifty way to add to your income is to invite that guest expert to host a workshop, demonstration, or lecture. It takes some of the pressure off you, gives your

---

Pricing a Workshop

Workshop Project: _____

Material	Retail Price
_____	_____
_____	_____
_____	_____
_____	_____
_____	_____
_____	_____
_____	_____
Materials total	_____
Expert's fee or employee wages	_____
Divide by number of expected participants	_____
Fee or wage total	_____
Total Cost of Workshop Per Participant	$ _____

---

customers fresh insights and new reasons to attend the event, and gives your guest expert a new customer base, as well as a reason to reciprocate and host you!

Ask an expert on culinary herbs, medicinal botanicals, herb crafts, or gardening with herbs to take on a demonstration or lecture. Most people—especially if they've recently written a book that needs to be promoted—will be delighted. You're offering free publicity! Keep in mind, however, that if your author or other expert doesn't live in your area, you may need to provide an honorarium or fee to compensate them for travel and lodging expenses. If you think your business can absorb this cost and still make a profit, fine. Otherwise, invite that expert to appear when he or she will already be in town.

And, of course, make sure that the topic of your guest's program is available through you. Have in stock those culinary or medicinal herbs, books on the subject, and other inventory to match the topic at hand. As with workshops, make sure you charge enough money per participant to cover any fees, including advertising. It's also perfectly acceptable to mark up your costs somewhat so the house (that's you) makes a profit. But, as always, do your market research to find out what fees your market will bear.

Whether for your own workshops, demonstrations, and seminars or for those given by guest experts, publicity is the key. If you don't tout the event, you won't get customers. Send out press releases to local media and fliers to customers, and place ads where they'll work for you.

14

Farmer's Almanac
Tales from the Trenches

As you now know from reading this book, starting an herb farm is not a formula for overnight success. You and your gardens can flourish, but only if you're willing to apply a combination of sheer physical labor, wise money management, savvy sales and marketing, and of course, a love of working the soil and tending nature's bounty. You'll also need

▲

to do lots of market research and loads of planning, keep learning all you can about herbs, share that knowledge with your customers, and be prepared to go with the flow as the market changes.

To help you with all of the above, we asked the herb farmers interviewed for this book for tips on spreading your roots as an herb farmer. Read on for their words of wisdom:

The Thoughtful Farmer

"Decide which aspects of the business you intend to concentrate on," advises herb farmer and herb association vice president Cindy M. in Hallettsville, Texas. "Do you want to grow fresh-cut, retail potted stock, or wholesale potted stock, plugs, or liners? Check out your markets. Are the local nurseries already well-stocked with a good selection of herbs, or is there a niche for you somewhere? It's important to try to see where you'll fit into the business in your area before you invest your own or someone

Risky Business?

As you set out to translate everything you've learned in this book into a thriving herb business, here are seven tips to take back to the farm with you:

1. *Read everything you can find about herbs*—how to grow them, what they're used for, and all their various medicinal and aesthetic uses. Even if you don't plan to specialize in some of these niches, you're an herb ambassador and will need to have a background in them all.

2. *Read some more!* Dig into everything you can find on starting and operating a small business.

3. *Don't skimp on the market research.* Plan your herb garden and your herbal business with care.

4. *Attend lectures and workshops and join local, regional, and national associations.* Find a mentor or two, and don't be afraid to ask questions.

5. *Mentor your customers.* Educate them in herbal care and lore. Teach them to share in the herbal revolution.

6. *Take advantage of publicity and PR.* Follow up on all leads, and be sure to thank sources who highlight your company.

7. *Have fun.* It's one of the perks of the job!

else's money. Talk to people, join a local herb organization if there is one, and check out the Internet for herb associations.

"Most of all, if you're going into the business because you love plants, think twice or thrice about whether you really want this to be a business at all. Plants take a great amount of time and care, and they don't make you any money sitting in your greenhouse. Have a plan to sell your product."

And that's not all. "If you think you'll cash in on the medicinal herbal revolution," the specialist in unusual herbs says, "do your homework extra hard. Find out what buyers want before you plow up that corn field to plant five acres of echinacea or evening primrose. Many medicinal herbs take several years in the field to reach a maturity that is usable in the trade. In my opinion, there is no get-rich-quick plan for an herb business, whether you're interested in field-grown herbs, a retail nursery, wholesale, or whatever. It's a lot of hard work and planning."

Ralph C. in Elizabethtown, Pennsylvania, agrees. "Plan on being very persistent," he says. "You'll quickly go from the beginner's luck stage to the reality stage, which is not quite as much fun and as easy as you thought."

So how do you compensate for reality? "Keep your eyes open and be ready to change," counsels Ralph, who at one time in his farm career segued from suddenly overmarketed dried flowers to a new line of fresh-cut flowers delivered to florist wholesalers. "Follow the need, then try to plug the hole. If 30 customers ask if you're open Friday evenings, for instance, say yes, even if you'd rather be home watching TV."

The Waiting Game

Patience and perseverance are the watchwords of the herb farm game, advises Michele B. in Soddy Daisy, Tennessee. "Expect downtime and slow time," she says. "During the heat of summer, don't expect much to happen—but watch out in the fall. We had our best month in September, not May like you'd think. Caught me by surprise!

"Always have on hand at least a few of everything you advertise. No one likes to be told you're out of something. But you can't always tell what people are going to want, and running out does happen. Learn how to advertise as inexpensively as possible—business cards, fliers, booklets that you write yourself, a really good informative catalog—and learn Web design. I taught myself, which saved a lot of money in the long run."

Being prepared also means covering your regulatory bases. "Talk to your local health inspector," says Donna F. in Midland, Michigan. When she started her business, she got an attorney who helped her meet zoning requirements for her home-based company, then helped her contact the health authorities.

"We met with the health inspector and went over the premises," Donna recalls. "He gave me a lot of ideas. My current inspector is also wonderful and has become a friend as well. You think of them as an enemy with beady eyes, but they're the best asset you can have. They can tell you regulations and help you in every aspect."

The Best of Times, the Worst of Times

None of the herb farmers interviewed for this book seems to have any intention of giving in and going corporate. They like what they're doing and how they're doing it and plan to keep on gardening. But can it all be fair skies and fragrant herbs? Even the most experienced and successful herb farmers must hit the occasional weed patch. To find out about more about the ups and downs, we asked our interviewees about their worst—and best—experiences in the business.

Weathering the Storm

"My worst farming experience had to be when temperatures here in Texas reached over 100 degrees for days on end," says Cindy. "I lost a lot of stock due to heat and humidity. Then, if that wasn't bad enough, I inadvertently left the gate to the pasture open and then left for about three hours. When I returned, cows were wandering through my growing area munching on lemon grass, purple fountain grass, evening primrose, and peppers. They had not gone into the greenhouse, much to my relief, but their big feet had done a job in the display gardens!"

Ralph says droughts—of which he's weathered two in 16 years—were the culprits responsible for his worst farming experiences, along with a tailwind from a hurricane that knocked down his tall crops. And to make matters worse, those crops were already sold under contract—and only 25 percent were deliverable after the storm.

Leaping Over Hurdles

Michele counts shipping as her worst herb farming experience. "We learned by trial and error how to pack our plants after several failures," she says. "We had to reship several plants to customers due to pots breaking, plants falling out of pots, etc. We've since learned a wonderful method from another herb farmer and have been successful ever since." Mike and Jadyne R., the lavender growers in Sequim, Washington, relate a shipping nightmare of another sort as their worst experience. "When we first started, we purchased a whole bunch of one lavender variety based on recommendations from the nursery," Mike recalls. "We planted them, and they grew like mad. We hired a bunch of people to help harvest and gently put them in gorgeous arrangements to dry. The orders came in, and we began shipping them off. The first person to receive an order called and said, 'The lavender smells great, but all the flowers are off the stem in the bottom of

Fun Fact

In the Middle Ages, laundry women were called "lavenders" because they tucked lavender in among cleaned and folded garments.

Smart Tip

Keep in mind that your customers and your community
are closely intertwined. "I think
community is where you
develop your power base," says
Mike R. in Sequim, Washington.
"If you take care of the community, it takes care of you." As a
measure of its involvement,
Mike's lavender farm throws a
barbecue for the town each year.
Elizabeth, Pennsylvania, farmer
Ralph C. does the same for his
employees.

the box.' We did more research and found that this variety didn't hold flowers on stems. We were just devastated."

Creativity saved the day. Jadyne developed a dozen or so lavender recipes, and the couple packaged up the recipes in a booklet and attached a sample of the blossoms removed from their stems. The disaster proved to be an instant winner. "They go out of here by the thousands," Mike says. "It's one of our bestsellers."

"I don't have to think twice to come up with my worst experience in the business," says Donna, who vividly recalls having to change her company name. It all started at a natural foods expo in Washington, DC, when she crossed paths with a California firm that had the same herbal name. The West Coast group, which had national sales at a time when Donna did not, forced her to change names. "That was my identity," she says. "It was like being told I couldn't be called Donna anymore."

Donna bounced back. She held a "Help Name the Herbary" contest, then got her company—under its new name—a registered trademark.

Reaping the Rewards

But herb farming certainly isn't all drought and disaster. Our entrepreneurs had no difficulties coming up with rewarding moments in their businesses.

"We've been so fortunate," says Mike. "I feel real lucky to be where I am. Our best experience so far is being picked up by HGTV's program "The Good Life.""

Mike rented a local casino for the episode's debut showing and invited the entire community to come watch on the big screen. "It was very exciting," he remembers. "Hundreds and hundreds of people came in. Thirty minutes after it was over, we turned on our Web site and watched the e-mail orders coming in—at the rate of one every two seconds. It continued for weeks, hundreds and hundreds and hundreds of orders every week. That's put us over the edge."

Ralph set out to achieve two goals when he started his company: to sell quality dried flowers at reasonable prices and to get the best from his employees without treating them

Fun Fact

The cooked roots of the perennial herb marsh mallow were once used to produce—you guessed it—marshmallow candy.

badly. And the latter he counts as his best experience in the business—the satisfaction of a good crew that stays with his farm, some for more than ten years, and has fun while they're at it. "We're friends," Ralph says.

Donna gives lots of herb lectures. As a home economics teacher, she's not nervous; she's used to speaking in front of people. But she's also not bored. "I get enthusiastic about doing this," she confesses. And she counts the results of one particular talk, about cooking with herbs, as her best experience in the business.

"A lady came up to me and said she had a 'new' kitchen that was three years old and had never been used," Donna remembers. "Then she said, 'I'm so excited! I can't wait to get home and get out my pots and pans. You've inspired me.' That can keep you going for a long time, to have an impact on people's lives—it's a personal connection."

Back to Nature

"My best farming experience has to be each spring," Cindy says, "when the plants look their best. New basils, marjorams, lemon balm, and the rest are all so green and lush. People are excited about a new growing season. There's that look in their eyes of hope and growth. They can just see their beautiful gardens. That's the feeling I like to promote in my customers. I do everything I can to help them achieve the gardens they see in their minds."

"The best herb farming experience?" asks Michele. "There are several. The most important is leaving the rat race behind every day and going into the gardens and greenhouse and seeing all those wonderful plants, touching them, smelling, and tasting. The next best is all the people we've met over the past few years and all the information we've gained from them.

"We have what I think is a really good thing going here. We provide something wonderful for people to nurture, and at the same time we're nurturing ourselves. Herbs do make the difference!"

It's up to You

As we explored at the outset of this book, it takes a certain personality to become a successful herb farmer. You have to be able to meld a down-to-earth, back-to-nature mellowness with a cutting-edge marketing mindset. If this describes you, you'll probably thrive. If not, you may come to the realization sooner or later that instead of living in the Garden of Eden, you're crawling through a bed of weeds. You're just not happy.

"Don't be afraid to take a risk," advises Mike. "If you are, your dream will never happen. Live out on the edge a little and take a chance. The biggest mistake is your fear of making one. If you're afraid of making mistakes—which you will—you'll never get ahead. Take the chance; use some good, clear, creative energy—and go for it."

If you, too, decide to grow for it and become an herb farmer, you'll harvest your own worst and best experiences to share. That's a part of nature and a part of life.

But if you go into it with the right ingredients: a fertile mind, as well as fertile soil, a willingness to work hard and to learn everything you can, the confidence to promote yourself and your herb products, and the drive to succeed, chances are you will.

Appendix
Herbal Entrepreneur's Storehouse

The quintessential storehouse for the successful herb farmer is filled not just with old seed packets, bags of potting soil, and well-oiled tools, but with a wealth of resources—a master list of places to go and people to contact for information on everything from industry associations and regulatory agencies to seed suppliers. We've compiled a list of resources to get you started stockpiling your own information storehouse.

These sources, however, are only the beginning. They are by no means the sole sources out there, and they should not be taken as the Ultimate Answer. We've done our research, but businesses—like people—tend to move, change, fold, and expand. So as we've repeatedly stressed, do your homework. Get out and get investigating, and add to this list as you go. Don't be afraid to ask questions. You'll be amazed at how much you'll learn.

Associations

American Botanical Council, P.O. Box 144345, Austin, TX 78714-4345, (512) 926-4900, www.herbalgram.org

American Herb Association, P.O. Box 1673, Nevada City, CA 95959, (530) 265-9552, www.jps.net/ahaherb

American Herbalists Guild, 1931 Gaddis Rd., Canton, GA 30115, (770) 751-6021, www.healthy.net/herbalists

American Herbal Products Association, 8484 Georgia Ave., #370, Silver Spring, MD 20910, (301) 588-1171, www.ahpa.org

Association of Crafts and Creative Industries, P.O. Box 3388, Zanesville, OH 43702-3388, (740) 452-4541, www.creative-industries.com

Herb & Botanical Alliance, 5916 Duerer St., P.O. Box 93, Egg Harbor City, NJ 08215, (609) 965-0337, www.expresspages.com/h/herbbotanical

Herb Growing and Marketing Network, P.O. Box 245, Silver Spring, PA 17575-0245, (717) 393-3295, www.herbworld.com

International Herb Association, 910 Charles St., Fredericksburg, VA 22401, (540) 368-0590, www.iherb.org

National Association for Holistic Aromatherapy, 2000 Second Ave., #206, Seattle, WA 98121, (888) ASK-NAHA, www.naha.org

National Association for the Specialty Food Trade, (212) 482-6440, www.specialty-food.com

National Craft Association, 1945 E. Ridge Rd., #5178, Rochester, NY 14622-2467, (800) 715-9594, (716) 266-5472, www.craftassoc.com

National Mail Order Association, 2807 Polk St. N.E., Minneapolis, MN 55418-2954, (888) 496-7337 (for ordering books and reports only), (612) 788-1673 www.nmoa.org

Texas Herb Growers and Marketers Association, c/o Cindy Meredith, The Herb Cottage, 442 CR 233, Hallettsville, TX 77964, (979) 562-2153, www.thgma.com

Beneficial Insects

The Beneficial Insect Co., P.O. Box 119, Glendale Springs, NC 28629, (336) 973-8490, www.thebeneficialinsectco.com

Nature's Control, (541) 245-6033, www.naturescontrol.com

Books

Backyard Market Gardening: The Entrepreneur's Guide to Selling What You Grow, by Andrew W. Lee, Good Earth Publications

The Bargain Hunter's Handbook: How to Buy Almost Anything for Next to Nothing, by Rob and Terry Adams, Career Press

The Book of Herbal Teas: A Guide to Gathering, Brewing and Drinking, by Sara Perry, Chronicle Books

The Encyclopedia of Popular Herbs: Your Complete Guide to the Leading Medicinal Plants, by Robert S. McCaleb, Evelyn Leigh, and Krisa Morien, Prima Health

Entrepreneur's business start-up guides:
- *Start Your Own Craft Business*
- *Start Your Own Mail Order Business*
- *Start Your Own Retail Store*
- *Start Your Own Seminar Production Business*

Growing and Selling Fresh-Cut Herbs, by Sandie Shores, Storey Books

Growing Your Herb Business, by Bertha Repert, Storey Books

Health and Beauty the Natural Way, by Nerys Purchon, Metro Books

Herbs for Sale: Growing and Marketing Herbs, Herbal Products, and Herbal Know-How, by Lee Sturdivant, San Juan Naturals

Medicinal Herbs in the Garden, Field & Marketplace, by Lee Sturdivant and Tim Blakley, San Juan Naturals

Profits from Your Backyard Herb Garden, by Lee Sturdivant, San Juan Naturals

Rodale's Illustrated Encyclopedia of Herbs, by Claire Kowalchik, Rodale Press

Rodale's Successful Herb Gardening, by Patricia S. Michalak, Rodale Press

Sell What You Grow: How to Take Your Herbs & Produce to Market for Serious Cash, by Mimi Luebbermann, Prima Publishing

Soapmaking for Fun & Profit, by Maria Given Nerius, Prima Home

Well Being: Rejuvenating Recipes for Body and Soul, by Barbara Close, Chronicle Books

Bottling and Packaging Supplies

Maxland International Inc., 9457 E. Rush St., S. El Monte, CA 91733, (626) 443-2443, www.maxland.com

Schilling Paper Co., P.O. Box 369, LaCrosse, WI 54602, (800) 888-1885, www.schillingpaper.com

Skywell Systems Inc., 213 W. Butler Ave., Ambler, PA 19002, (800) 220-9770, www.skywell.com

Snowdrift Farm Natural Products Inc., 3759 N. Romero Rd., #141, Tucson, AZ 85705, (888) 999-6950, (520) 407-8370, www.snowdriftfarm.com

Sunburst Bottle Co., 5710 Auburn Blvd., #7, Sacramento, CA 95841, (916) 348-5576, www.sunburstbottle.com

Consultants

Paul Mertel, The Herb Merchant, 7072 W. Pomfret St., Carlisle, PA 17013, (717) 249-0970

Mike Reichner, Purple Haze Lavender Farm, 180 Bell Bottom Rd., Sequim, WA 98382, (888) 852-6560, (360) 683-1714, www.purplehazelavender.com

Cyber Assistance

The Chamomile Times and Herbal News, www.chamomiletimes.com

China Bayles Herbal Mysteries, www.mysterypartners.com, lots of herbal tips and recipes from the author of this renowned mystery series

Garden Guides, www.gardenguides.com/herbs, just what it says, an online guide to herbs

GardenWeb, www.gardenweb.com, a bevy of gardening forums, seed and plant exchanges, tips and advice, dictionary, glossary, and more

The GreenBeam, www.greenbeam.com, bills itself as "the online channel for horticulture business solutions"

WebGarden, http://webgarden.osu.edu, scads of resources for gardening and horticultural professionals, from novice to old pro

Essential Oil and Soap-Making Supplies

Amaranthine Aromatics, 4429 Hillcroft Dr., Cleveland, OH 44128, (800) 842-8609, www.aaroma.com

Camden-Grey Essential Oils, 7178-A SW 47 St., Miami, FL 33155, (877) 232-7662, (305) 740-3494, www.essentialoil.net

Naturopathica, (800) 669-7618, www.naturopathica.com

Sabia, 500 N. Lamar, #150, Austin, TX 78703, (888) SABIA77, (512) 469-0447, www.sabia.com

Snowdrift Farm Natural Products Inc., 3759 N. Romero Rd., #141, Tucson, AZ 85705, (888) 999-6950, (520) 407-8370, www.snowdriftfarm.com

Wholesale Supplies Plus.com Inc., (800) 359-0944, (440) 582-5620 (in Ohio), www.wholesalesuppliesplus.com

Farmers' Markets

AMS Farmers Markets, www.ams.usda.gov/farmersmarkets

Greenmarket Program, Council on the Environment of New York City, (212) 788-7900, http://users.rcn.com/conyc

Palm Beach County Green Markets, Palm Beach County Cooperative Extension Service-Agricultural Economic Development, (561) 233-1792, www.co.palm-beach.fl.us/greenmar

Note: Check with your local city or county for information on farmers' or green markets in your area.

Greenhouses and Greenhouse Accessories

Charley's Greenhouse Supply, 17979 State Rte. 536, Mount Vernon, WA 98273-3269, (800) 322-4707, www.charleysgreenhouse.com

Gardener's Supply Co., 128 Intervale Rd., Burlington, VT 05401-2850, (800) 863-1700, www.gardeners.com

The Yard Works, 15919 Hwy. 99, Lynwood, WA 98037, (800) 369-8333, www.yardworks-greenhouses.com

Growing Supplies

American Plant Products & Services Inc., 9200 N.W. 10th, Oklahoma City, OK 73127, (800) 522-3376, (405) 787-4833, www.americanplant.com

A Gardener's Resource, P.O. Box 85072, Tucson, AZ 85754, (520) 792-8023, www.agardenersresource.com, prices here are higher, but you're not tied to a high-quantity order as with some other wholesale suppliers

Orion Industries, 233 Chablis Wy., Cloverdale, CA 95425, (707) 529-8707, www.gardenmarker.com

Teufel Nursery, 12345 N.W. Barnes Rd., Portland, OR 97229, (800) 483-8335, (503) 646-1111, www.teufel.com

Helpful Government Agencies

Agricultural Marketing Service, www.ams.usda.gov

Bureau of the Census, www.census.gov

U.S. Department of Agriculture, www.usda.gov

▲

U.S. Food and Drug Administration, www.fda.gov

U.S. Postal Service, www.usps.com

Note: Be sure to contact your own state department of agriculture and local health department for any rules and regulations you may need to know.

Irrigation Systems

Berry Hill Irrigation, 3744 Hwy. 58, Buffalo Jct., VA 24529, (800) 345-3747, (804) 374-5555, www.berryhilldrip.com

DripWorks, 190 Sanhedrin Cr., Willits, CA 95490-8753, (800) 522-3747 (for orders), (707) 459-6323, www.dripworksusa.com

Magazines and Publications

Business Start-Up Kit, available from the Herb Growing and Marketing Network by mail or download, www.herbworld.com

The Growing Edge, P.O. Box 1027, Corvallis, OR 97339-1027, (800) 888-6785, www.growingedge.com

Herbs at Home, P.O. Box 5225, Kendallville, IN 46755, (877) 843-4372, www.herbsat homemagazine.com

The Herb Companion, www.discoverherbs.com

Herbs for Health, www.discoverherbs.com

Organic Gardening, www.organicgardening.com

Schools and Classes

Check out more learning resources than you can imagine online on the Herb Growing and Marketing Network's "University" site at www.herbnet.com/university_p2.htm

Seed and Plant Suppliers

Johnny's Selected Seeds, 1 Foss Hill Rd., RR 1, Box 2580, Albion, ME 04910-9731, (207) 437-4301, www.johnnyseeds.com

The Herb Cottage, Cindy Meredith, 442 CR 233, Hallettsville, TX 77964, (979) 562-2153, www.theherbcottage.com

Nichols Garden Nursery, 1190 Old Salem Rd. NE, Albany, OR 97321, (541) 928-9280, www.nicholsgardennursery.com

Papa Geno's Herb Farm, 11125 S. 14th St., Roca, NE 68430, (402) 423-5051, www.papagenos.com

Possum Creek Herb Farm, Michele and Scott Brown, 528 Nature Trail, Soddy Daisy, TN 37379, (423) 332-0347, www.possumcreekherb.com

Richters Herb Specialists, 357 Hwy. 47, Goodwood, ON, LOC 1A0, CAN, (905) 640-6677, www.richters.com

Victory Seeds, P.O. Box 192, Molalla, OR 97038, (503) 829-3126, www.victoryseeds.com

Shipping Supplies

Anchor Box Co., 5889 S. Gessner Rd., Houston, TX 77036, (800) 522-8820, (713) 778-1500, www.anchorbox.com

Associated Bag Co., 400 W. Boden St., Milwaukee, WI 53207-0120, (800) 926-6100, www.associatedbag.com

Successful Herb Farm Businesses

Cramers' Posie Patch, Ralph Cramer, 116 Trail Rd N., Elizabethtown, PA 17022, (877) CRAMERS, www.cramersposiepatch.com

Frawley's Fine Herbary, Donna Frawley, 4613 Lund Dr., Midland, MI 48642, (517) 631-3136, e-mail: frawleyherbs@a1access.net

The Herb Cottage, Cindy Meredith, 442 CR 233, Hallettsville, TX 77964, (979) 562-2153, e-mail: herbs@theherbcottage.com, www.theherbcottage.com

Possum Creek Herb Farm, Michele and Scott Brown, 528 Nature Trail, Soddy Daisy, TN 37379, (423) 332-0347, e-mail: poscreek@bellsouth.net, www.possumcreekherb. com

Purple Haze Lavender Farm, Mike and Jadyne Reichner, 180 Bell Bottom Rd., Sequim, WA 98382, (888) 852-6560, (360) 683-1714, e-mail: info@purplehazelavender.com, www.purplehazelavender.com

Weight Scales

Itin Scale Co. Inc., 433 Ave. U, Brooklyn, NY 11223, (718) 336-5900, www.itinscales.com

Precision Weighing Balances, 10 Peabody St., Bradford, MA 01835-7614, (800) 881-9570 (for orders only), (978) 521-7095, www.balances.com

Glossary

Annual: plant that matures, flowers, and dies in a single growing season.

Aromatherapy: art and science of using botanical scents for healing.

Attar of roses: rose essential oil.

Ayurveda: ancient Hindu system of medicine and longevity now seeing a resurgence in modern life.

Bath bag: a tea bag for the bath.

Biennial: plant that produces leaves in its first growing season, then flowers and dies after its second season.

Carrier oil: a vegetable, nut, or seed oil used to dilute the strength of essential oils.

Cold process: soap-making method involving the use of sodium hydroxide.

Compost: organic vegetable waste deliberately decomposed into loam.

Cultivar: cultivated variety of a plant.

Decoction: an extract made by simmering raw ingredients like bark and roots in boiling water.

▲

Display garden: garden designed for visitors—and potential herb buyers—to tour for enjoyment, as well as gain knowledge of how mature plants look in the landscape during different seasons and in conjunction with other growing herbs.

Dream pillow: pillow into which herbs that promote pleasant dreams are sewn.

Drip irrigation: irrigation system that uses poly tubing studded with drip or bubble nozzles and misters.

Encarsia formosa: wasplike insect used as beneficial pest control.

Essential oil: a distilled plant essence.

Everlastings: dried flowers.

Fixative: dried botanical used to fix the scent in potpourri.

Hand-milling: method for creating soap from a premade base.

Hardening off: practice of placing greenhouse or indoor-grown seedlings outdoors for consecutively longer periods to acclimate them to outdoor temperatures.

Herbal: book dedicated to the description of herbs and their uses, usually in medicinal contexts.

Herbal vinegar: culinary or cosmetic vinegar made by steeping fresh herbs in vinegar.

Herbs: the leaves or other parts of temperate-climate plants.

Herb water: an infusion for external use.

Infused oil: oil made by steeping fresh herbs in oil.

Infusion: A tea that is steeped for as long as several hours.

Liner: small starter-sized plant, one size larger than a plug.

Melt-and-pour: a soap-making method using a premade base.

Ooze irrigation: irrigation system that uses recycled rubber hoses that ooze water.

OTC drug: drug that is sold over the counter; a nonprescription drug.

Perennial: plant that grows for years as opposed to short-lived annuals and biennials.

Perlite: volcanic glass used as a potting medium.

Physick garden: garden in which medicinal herbs were cultivated during the Middle Ages and later periods.

Phytomedicine: medicine derived from botanicals.

Plug: smallest starter-sized plant with a not-yet-established root system.

Pomander ball: citrus fruit studded with cloves and sometimes dusted with spices.

Potpourri: a mix of dried botanicals and essential oils used to scent a room.

Sachet: potpourri that is ground or crumbled and sewn into a fabric pouch.

Sleep pillow: pillow into which sleep-inducing herbs are sewn.

Sodium hydroxide: a chemical used in making soap.

Spices: the seeds, bark, or other parts of tropical plants.

Stillroom: a room for the distilling or other preparation of herbal remedies.

Synergy: custom blend of various essential oils formulated for a specific purpose.

TAP: see True aromatherapy product.

Tea: beverage made by steeping leaves, flowers, or stems in boiled water.

Tincture: an extract made by steeping an herb in vodka or other ingestible alcohol.

Tisane: another word for tea, or a very strong tea.

True aromatherapy product (TAP): an unadulterated essential oil as opposed to a fragrance oil derived from petrochemicals.

Wildcraft: to forage for wild botanicals.

Index

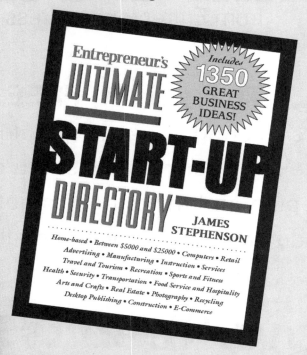